easy healthy dinners

GRAND AVENUE
BOOKS

Grand Avenue Books

An imprint of Meredith® Corporation

Easy Healthy Dinners

Contributing Editors: Sharyl Heiken, Rosemary Hutchinson (Spectrum Communication Services)

Contributing Designer: Joline Rivera

Copy and Production Editor: Victoria Forlini

Copy Chief: Terri Fredrickson

Contributing Proofreaders: David Craft, Maria Duryée, Sheila Mauck

Editorial Operations Manager: Karen Schirm

Manager, Book Production: Rick von Holdt

Editorial and Design Assistants: Karen McFadden, Mary Lee Gavin, Patricia Loder

Grand Avenue Books

Editor In Chief: Linda Raglan Cunningham

Design Director: Matt Strelecki

Executive Editor, Grand Avenue Books: Dan Rosenberg

Publisher: James D. Blume

Executive Director, Marketing: Jeffrey Myers

Executive Director, New Business Development: Todd M. Davis

Executive Director, Sales: Ken Zagor

Director, Operations: George A. Susral

Director, Production: Douglas M. Johnston

Business Director: Jim Leonard

Vice President and General Manager: Douglas J. Guendel

Meredith Publishing Group

President, Publishing Group: Stephen M. Lacy

Vice President-Publishing Director: Bob Mate

Meredith Corporation

Chairman and Chief Executive Officer: William T. Kerr

In Memoriam: E.T. Meredith III (1933-2003)

Library of Congress Control Number: 2002111434

ISBN: 0-696-21684-1

All of us at Grand Avenue Books are dedicated to providing you with the information and ideas you need to create delicious foods. We welcome your comments and suggestions. Write to us at: Grand Avenue Books, Editorial Department LN-114, 1716 Locust Street, Des Moines, IA 50309-3023

Pictured on front cover: Molasses-Glazed Pork Tenderloin (see recipe, page 42)

SMART EATING

You've promised yourself to start cooking more healthful meals so your family will feel better and live longer. But with a jam-packed schedule and a family that insists on great-tasting "real" food, your goal seems impossible. Does that sound familiar? Help is at hand. *Easy Healthy Dinners* brings you more than 100 recipes for terrific dishes that are high in flavor and taste appeal, but low in fat, calories, cholesterol, and sodium. Each has a complete nutrition analysis. And best of all, the recipes are made with easy-to-find ingredients and most go together in 30 minutes or less.

Tempt your family with enticing meat main dishes, such as Beef and Bean Burritos, Pork Medallions with Cherry Sauce, or Honey-Mustard Lamb Chops, and tantalizing poultry favorites, including Fried Chicken with Gravy, Chicken Fajitas, and Turkey and Nectarine Salad. Or if you prefer fish, seafood, or meatless entrées, sample Snapper Veracruz, Sautéed Shrimp with Peppers, or Southwestern Black Bean Cakes with Guacamole. To round out meals, opt for side dishes such as Caramelized Sweet Potatoes, Cream-Sauced Peas and Onions, and Fruited Spinach Salad with Currant Vinaigrette. And for dessert, select from Berry-Lemon Trifle, Chocolate Ricotta-Filled Pears, Tiramisu, and Gingered Peach and Pear Crisp.

Besides a selection of dynamite recipes, *Easy Healthy Dinners* also offers you practical pointers for making healthy cooking and eating a way of life.

Don't wait any longer—let *Easy Healthy Dinners* help you put your best intentions into action. Choose a recipe or two now and begin cooking more nutritious meals for your family tonight. You'll be amazed at how easy healthy cooking can be, and your family will applaud the delicious results.

Jamaican Pork and Sweet Potato Stir-Fry
(see recipe, page 64)

MAKING MEALS HEALTHIER

There's nothing magic about cooking delicious, full-flavored meals that are lower in calories, fat, and sodium. It's just a matter of making small changes.

Cooking more healthful meals for your family doesn't have to involve overhauling the way your family eats. It simply means adapting the dishes you love to use health-smart cooking techniques, replacing high-fat ingredients with lower-fat ones, and looking for fat-free ways to add flavor. Here are some suggestions.

Healthwise Cooking Hints

- Trim all visible fat from meat before cooking. Skin poultry and remove the underlying fat. Select water-pack tuna rather than the oil-pack type.
- Rely on cooking techniques that don't use added fat, such as broiling, grilling, poaching, steaming, and baking. For some of your favorite recipes that call for sautéing or pan-frying meat or poultry, try grilling or broiling instead.
- Make sautéing or stir-frying more healthful by using less fat. Use a nonstick skillet or wok and coat it with nonstick cooking spray or a small amount of butter, margarine, or cooking oil. If you use oil, opt for olive oil because health experts believe it helps lower blood cholesterol.
- Drain off extra fat from cooking pans before moving to the next recipe step.
- Use salt sparingly. Avoid adding salt during cooking. If needed, you can salt foods at the table with a low-sodium salt substitute. Rinse canned beans and vegetables to remove extra salt.
- Look for low-sodium vegetables and tomato products at the grocery store. Also take advantage of reduced-sodium chicken broth, lower-sodium beef broth, and lower-sodium soups.

Swapping Ingredients

- Limit the amount of meat in your meals. Use only 2 to 4 ounces per serving and add pasta, rice, grains, beans, or vegetables to round out the menu.
- Opt for meats that look lean without a lot of visible fat. Cuts labeled "loin" or "round" are good choices.
- Try using ground turkey or chicken breast instead of ground beef or pork in casseroles, chili, sloppy joes, pizza, meatballs, or meat loaf.
- If a recipe calls for sausage, bacon, or ham, look for the turkey-based version. It often will have fewer calories and less saturated fat. You also can substitute lean smoked ham for bacon.
- When it comes to condiments and dairy products—such as mayonnaise, salad dressings, sour cream, yogurt, cheeses, and cream—there is often a reduced-fat or fat-free version you can use. Read the labels, however; these products are not always low calorie.

Learning From Labels

The labels on many food products tell a lot about the nutrition values of the items. Here's some of what you'll find on labels:

- The standard serving size listed on the Nutrition Facts panel determines the nutrient content of a serving. A standard serving must reflect the amount of an item that a person over 4 years old would eat.
- The government has strict rules for the use of the terms "fat free," "cholesterol free," and "light" on labels. For example, only foods that are at least 97% free of fat can use the term "fat free." Also, a product can be designated "cholesterol free" only if it contains no more than a specific (very low) amount of saturated fat.
- The figures for fat listed on the label include the amounts of total fat and saturated fat contained in a serving. They are listed both in grams and as "% daily value." The daily value percentages tell you how much the fat in a serving contributes to a daily diet of 2,000 calories.
- A product can claim "no sugars added" only if no sugar of any kind (including fructose, concentrated fruit juice, or other sugar-containing products) has been added during processing.

• As a beverage, replace whole milk with reduced-fat or fat-free milk. (You may want to do this in stages to give your family time to adjust to lower-fat milk.) And in sauces, soups, and baked items, reduced-fat or fat-free milk, buttermilk, and evaporated fat-free milk are great lower-fat options.

• To increase fiber in your meals, look for breads, crackers, and cereals that list whole grains or whole-grain flour as the first ingredient.

• For homemade breads and other baked goods, you can replace up to half of the all-purpose flour with whole wheat flour.

• Using grains, such as barley, brown rice, wild rice, and bulgur, as side dishes also will boost fiber. And whole wheat pasta, corn tortillas, rye crackers, and oatmeal are other fiber-rich choices.

• Include dark green, leafy vegetables, such as spinach, broccoli, Swiss chard, and kale, in salads, sandwiches, soups, and stir-fries.

• Don't forget the deep yellow fruits and vegetables, such as peaches, apricots, cantaloupes, carrots, sweet potatoes, and winter squashes. They're high in vitamin A.

• Include plenty of fresh, canned, frozen, or dried fruits in your meals. Add them to salads, cold pasta dishes, side dishes, casseroles, meat stuffings, and dips. Pureed fruits make great low-calorie, low-fat sauces for roasts or chops. Select canned fruits packed in their own juices rather than heavy syrup. Or buy loose-pack frozen fruits with no added sugar or syrup.

• To lower the fat and cholesterol in recipes such as omelets and baked goods, use an egg substitute in place of the eggs. Or you can replace 1 whole egg in a recipe with 2 egg whites.

Adding Flavor the Low-Fat Way

The next time plain vegetables, meat, poultry, or fish need a flavor boost, don't rely on an extra pat of butter or sprinkling of salt. Instead, perk them up with one of these healthwise seasoning options:

• **Fresh and dried herbs.** Use them in recipes of all kinds. They work especially well in salad dressings, marinades, and sauces.

• **Dried herb mixtures.** Seasoning blends such as fines herbes, Cajun seasoning, five-spice powder, jerk seasoning, pumpkin pie spice, and apple pie spice save time and money and add lots of great flavor.

• **Flavored pepper seasonings.** Sprinkle on the likes of lemon-pepper seasoning, garlic pepper, or herb pepper.

• **Citrus peel and juices.** Grated fresh lemon, lime, or orange peel adds pizzazz to vegetables, salad dressings, whole-grain dishes, baked goods, and desserts. Lemon, lime, and orange juices are ideal for fish, pasta, salad dressings, and dessert sauces.

• **Grated fresh ginger.** Add a small amount (start with 1/2 teaspoon) of peeled and grated gingerroot to either sweet or savory dishes.

• **Roasted garlic.** Add cloves of mild, smooth roasted garlic to main dishes and cooked vegetables or use as a spread on bread for an appetizer. To roast a head of garlic, cut off the pointed top and place the head, cut side up, in a baking dish. Drizzle it with a little olive oil. Cover and bake the head in a 400°F oven about 25 minutes or until the cloves are soft.

• **Roasted red sweet peppers.** These smoky peppers are sold bottled in the produce section of the supermarket. They add a hint of sophistication to appetizers, main dishes, and salads.

• **Green onions, leeks, and shallots.** Sliced raw, they make great additions to salads and pizzas. Sautéed, they rev up main dishes and soups.

• **Bottled pepper sauces and salsas.** Ranging from mild to fiery, these condiments can spice up soups, gravies, and sauces. Salsa makes a great sauce for pizza or pasta too.

• **Mustards.** There's a wide variety to choose from—including honey, spicy, coarse-grain brown, herb, peppercorn, sweet-hot, hickory, and Chinese.

• **Chutneys.** Available in flavors such as mango, peach, or pear, these fruit medleys are just right served with grilled or broiled meat, poultry, or fish.

• **Light soy or teriyaki sauces.** Cut the sodium in marinades and sauces with these lively mixtures.

• **Flavored vinegars.** These zesty combinations can add a flavor jolt to just about any recipe that calls for vinegar. You'll find herbed, balsamic, champagne, fruit, and wine versions.

• **Pungent cheeses.** Just a sprinkling of Parmesan or Romano cheese, blue cheese, sharp cheddar, feta cheese, or goat cheese adds a bold accent to salads, soups, and sauces.

MEATS

Rely on these irresistible beef, veal, pork, and lamb recipes as the building blocks for healthful meals.

Steak Salad with Buttermilk Dressing
(see recipe, page 27)

FLANK STEAK WITH PINEAPPLE SALSA

The easy fruit salsa starts with a base of green picante sauce and ends with colorful bits of pineapple, orange, and sweet pepper.

Start to Finish: 20 minutes **Makes:** 4 servings

- **2 cups chopped, peeled, and cored fresh pineapple**
- **1 11-ounce can mandarin orange sections, drained**
- **1/2 cup chopped red or green sweet pepper**
- **1/3 cup mild green picante sauce or green taco sauce**
- **12 ounces beef flank or boneless beef sirloin steak, cut 1/2 inch thick**
- **1/2 teaspoon Mexican seasoning or chili powder**
- **1 tablespoon olive oil**
- **4 to 6 cups packaged torn mixed salad greens**

1

For pineapple salsa, in a medium bowl gently stir together pineapple, mandarin oranges, sweet pepper, and picante sauce or taco sauce. Set aside.

2

Trim fat from steak. Thinly slice steak across the grain. Sprinkle with Mexican seasoning or chili powder; toss to coat evenly. In a large skillet heat oil. Cook and stir half of the seasoned steak in hot oil over medium-high heat for 2 to 3 minutes or until done. Remove from skillet. Repeat with remaining steak.

3

To serve, arrange salad greens on plates. Top with steak and pineapple salsa.

Nutrition Facts per serving: 245 calories, 10 g total fat, 40 mg cholesterol, 224 mg sodium, 23 g carbohydrate, 18 g protein.

SOUTHWEST BEEF AND LINGUINE TOSS

Picante sauce makes an easy and flavorful stir-fry sauce for this Tex-Mex pasta.

Start to Finish: 25 minutes **Makes:** 4 servings

- **4 ounces dried linguine**
- **12 ounces beef top round steak**
- **1 tablespoon cooking oil**
- **2 teaspoons chili powder**
- **1/2 teaspoon bottled minced garlic or 1 clove garlic, minced**
- **1 small onion, sliced and separated into rings**
- **1 red or green sweet pepper, cut into thin, bite-size strips**
- **1 10-ounce package frozen whole kernel corn**
- **1/4 cup bottled picante sauce**
- **Fresh cilantro sprigs (optional)**
- **Chili powder (optional)**

1

Cook linguine according to package directions. Drain linguine. Rinse with warm water. Set aside.

2

Meanwhile, trim fat from steak. Cut steak into bite-size strips. Set aside.

3

Pour oil into a wok or large skillet. (Add more oil as necessary during cooking.) Heat over medium-high heat. Stir-fry the 2 teaspoons chili powder and the garlic in hot oil for 15 seconds. Add onion; stir-fry for 1 minute. Add the sweet pepper; stir-fry for 1 to 2 minutes more or until vegetables are crisp-tender. Remove vegetables from wok.

4

Add the steak strips to the hot wok; stir-fry for 2 to 3 minutes or until cooked through. Return vegetables to the wok. Stir in corn and picante sauce. Add the cooked linguine. Toss together to coat with sauce. Cook and stir until heated through. If desired, garnish with cilantro and sprinkle with additional chili powder.

Nutrition Facts per serving: 351 calories, 9 g total fat, 54 mg cholesterol, 166 mg sodium, 43 g carbohydrate, 27 g protein.

SMOTHERED STEAK WITH HONEYED RED ONIONS

When sweet Vidalia or Walla Walla onions are in season, use them instead of the red onion.

Start to Finish: 30 minutes **Makes:** 4 servings

- **1/3 cup red wine vinegar**
- **3 tablespoons honey**
- **1/2 teaspoon dried thyme, crushed**
- **1 large red onion, thinly sliced**
- **1 pound beef top loin or beef tenderloin steak, cut 1 inch thick**
- **1/2 teaspoon cracked black pepper**
- **2 tablespoons snipped fresh parsley**

1

In a medium bowl stir together the vinegar, honey, and thyme. Separate the onion slices; add to the vinegar mixture. Let stand while preparing beef; stir occasionally.

2

Meanwhile, trim fat from beef. Cut into serving-size pieces. Sprinkle both sides of steak pieces with pepper, pressing into the surface of beef.

3

In a large nonstick skillet cook steak pieces over medium-high heat for 10 minutes, turning once halfway through cooking. Remove from skillet.

4

Add the onion mixture to the drippings in skillet. Cook over medium heat for 3 to 4 minutes or until onion is just crisp-tender, stirring occasionally. Stir snipped parsley into onion mixture. Remove from skillet; keep warm.

5

Return steak pieces and any accumulated juices to skillet. Reduce heat to medium-low. Cook, uncovered, for 2 to 5 minutes or until juices are slightly reduced and steaks are medium doneness (160°), occasionally spooning the juices over the steaks.

6

To serve, transfer steak pieces to 4 dinner plates. Top with onion mixture.

Nutrition Facts per serving: 273 calories, 10 g total fat, 76 mg cholesterol, 59 mg sodium, 19 g carbohydrate, 26 g protein.

PEPPERED STEAK WITH MUSHROOM SAUCE

Green peppercorns, thyme, and oregano make this calorie-conscious main dish triple good.

Start to Finish: 30 minutes **Makes:** 6 servings

- **6 beef tenderloin steaks or 3 beef top sirloin steaks, cut 1 inch thick (about 1½ pounds total)**
- **1½ teaspoons dried whole green peppercorns, crushed, or ½ teaspoon coarsely ground black pepper**
- **½ teaspoon dried thyme, crushed**
- **½ teaspoon dried oregano, crushed**
- **¼ teaspoon salt**
- **Nonstick cooking spray**
- **⅓ cup water**
- **½ teaspoon instant beef bouillon granules**
- **¾ cup sliced fresh shiitake mushrooms or other fresh mushrooms**
- **¾ cup fat-free milk**
- **2 tablespoons all-purpose flour**
- **½ teaspoon dried thyme, crushed**
- **⅔ cup fat-free or light dairy sour cream**
- **1 tablespoon snipped fresh chives (optional)**

1

Trim fat from steaks. In a small bowl combine peppercorns or pepper, ½ teaspoon thyme, the oregano, and salt. Sprinkle both sides of steaks with mixture, pressing into meat.

2

Coat an unheated large nonstick skillet with nonstick cooking spray. Heat skillet over medium heat. Cook steaks in hot skillet for 10 to 13 minutes for medium doneness (160°), turning once halfway through cooking. Remove from skillet. Cover to keep warm.

3

Add the water and bouillon granules to skillet. Bring to boiling. Add mushrooms. Cook about 2 minutes or until tender. In a small bowl stir together milk, flour, and ½ teaspoon thyme. Add to skillet. Cook and stir until thickened and bubbly. Stir in sour cream; heat through, but do not boil.

4

To serve, spoon sauce over steaks. If desired, garnish with chives.

Nutrition Facts per serving: 206 calories, 7 g total fat, 64 mg cholesterol, 243 mg sodium, 9 g carbohydrate, 25 g protein.

HERBED STEAK

This no-fuss steak is especially delicious in the summer when fresh herbs and straight-from-the-garden tomatoes are plentiful.

Start to Finish: 25 minutes **Makes:** 4 servings

- **2 beef top loin steaks, cut 3/4 inch thick (about 1 1/4 pounds total)**
- **1 tablespoon margarine or butter**
- **3 green onions, sliced (about 1/3 cup)**
- **1 1/2 teaspoons snipped fresh basil or thyme or 1/2 teaspoon dried basil or thyme, crushed**
- **1/4 teaspoon salt**
- **1/8 teaspoon ground black pepper**
- **1 medium tomato, chopped**
- **Fresh basil or thyme sprigs (optional)**

1

Trim fat from steaks. Cut each steak in half. In a heavy, large skillet cook steaks in hot margarine or butter over medium heat to desired doneness [allow about 12 minutes for medium doneness (160°)], turning once halfway through cooking.

2

Remove steaks, reserving drippings in skillet. Cover steaks to keep warm. Cook green onions, snipped or dried herb, salt, and pepper in drippings for 1 to 2 minutes or until green onions are tender. Stir in tomato. Heat through.

3

To serve, spoon tomato mixture over steaks. If desired, garnish with herb sprigs.

Nutrition Facts per serving: 207 calories, 9 g total fat, 81 mg cholesterol, 230 mg sodium, 2 g carbohydrate, 28 g protein.

BEEF STEAK WITH RED ONION RELISH

All you need is 25 minutes and you can serve this impressive entrée to family or friends.

Start to Finish: 25 minutes **Makes:** 4 servings

- **1 pound boneless beef top sirloin steak, cut 3/4 inch thick**
- **1/4 to 1 teaspoon coarsely ground black pepper**
- **2 teaspoons cooking oil**
- **1 large red onion, thickly sliced and separated into rings**
- **1 7½-ounce can tomatoes, cut up**
- **1/4 cup dry red wine**
- **1/2 teaspoon dried sage, crushed**
- **1/4 teaspoon salt**

1

Trim fat from steak. Cut into 4 equal portions and rub both sides of each portion with pepper. In a large nonstick skillet heat oil over medium-high heat. Add steaks and cook about 13 minutes or until medium doneness (160°), turning once halfway through cooking. Remove steaks from skillet, reserving drippings in skillet. Keep steaks warm.

2

In the same skillet cook onion in drippings over medium heat for 5 to 7 minutes or until crisp-tender. Carefully add tomatoes, wine, sage, and salt. Bring to boiling. Cook for 1 to 2 minutes or until most of the liquid is evaporated, stirring occasionally.

3

To serve, arrange steaks on plates. Spoon onion mixture on top.

Nutrition Facts per serving: 246 calories, 12 g total fat, 76 mg cholesterol, 200 mg sodium, 3 g carbohydrate, 26 g protein.

BEEF WITH CUCUMBER RAITA

Raita is a cooling yogurt salad that helps counteract the heat of fiery Indian main dishes.

Start to Finish: 30 minutes **Makes:** 4 servings

- **1 8-ounce carton plain fat-free or low-fat yogurt**
- **1/4 cup coarsely shredded unpeeled cucumber**
- **1 tablespoon finely chopped red or sweet onion**
- **1 tablespoon snipped fresh mint**
- **1/4 teaspoon sugar**
- **Salt**
- **Ground black pepper**
- **1 pound boneless beef top sirloin steak, cut 1 inch thick**
- **1/2 teaspoon lemon-pepper seasoning**
- **Fresh mint leaves (optional)**

1

For raita, in a small bowl combine yogurt, cucumber, onion, snipped mint, and sugar. Season to taste with salt and pepper; set aside.

2

Trim fat from steak. Sprinkle steak with lemon-pepper seasoning. Place steak on the unheated rack of a broiler pan. Broil 3 to 4 inches from heat for 20 to 22 minutes or until medium doneness (160°), turning once halfway through broiling. Cut steak across the grain into thin slices. If desired, arrange steak slices on mint leaves. Top with raita.

Nutrition Facts per serving: 237 calories, 10 g total fat, 77 mg cholesterol, 235 mg sodium, 5 g carbohydrate, 29 g protein.

MEDITERRANEAN-STYLE BEEF STIR-FRY

To save time when making this Italian-accented stir-fry, start heating the water for the pasta before you do anything else.

Start to Finish: 30 minutes **Makes:** 4 servings

- **6 ounces dried fettuccine or linguine**
- **12 ounces boneless beef top round steak, cut 3/4 inch thick**
- **Nonstick cooking spray**
- **2 cloves garlic, minced**
- **1 medium yellow summer squash, halved and sliced diagonally**
- **2 cups fresh or frozen broccoli florets**
- **1 teaspoon cooking oil**
- **1 cup cherry tomato quarters**
- **4 green onions, sliced**
- **1/3 cup bottled reduced-calorie or fat-free Italian salad dressing**
- **1 tablespoon finely shredded Parmesan cheese**

1

Cook pasta according to package directions. Drain pasta. Return to pan. Cover; keep warm. Meanwhile, trim fat from steak. Thinly slice steak across the grain into bite-size strips. Coat an unheated wok or large skillet with nonstick cooking spray. Heat over medium heat. Stir-fry garlic in hot wok for 15 seconds. Add squash and broccoli; stir-fry for 4 to 5 minutes or until crisp-tender.

2

Remove vegetables from wok. Heat oil in wok. Stir-fry steak strips in hot oil for 3 to 4 minutes or until cooked through. Return vegetables to wok. Add cherry tomatoes, green onions, and salad dressing. Toss to mix. Cover and heat through.

3

To serve, spoon beef mixture over hot cooked pasta. Sprinkle with Parmesan cheese.

Nutrition Facts per serving: 371 calories, 9 g total fat, 57 mg cholesterol, 251 mg sodium, 43 g carbohydrate, 30 g protein.

SOUTHWEST SKILLET STEAKS

Starting with tenderized beef cubed steaks makes this Tex-Mex skillet meal quick and easy.

Start to Finish: 30 minutes **Makes:** 4 servings

- **1/4 cup all-purpose flour**
- **1/4 teaspoon garlic salt**
- **1/4 teaspoon ground cumin**
- **1/8 teaspoon ground red pepper**
- **4 4-ounce lean beef cubed steaks**
- **Nonstick cooking spray**
- **1 14 1/2-ounce can low-sodium tomatoes, cut up**
- **1 4-ounce can diced green chile peppers, drained**
- **1/3 cup low-sodium tomato paste (1/2 of a 6-ounce can)**
- **1 tablespoon snipped fresh oregano or 1 teaspoon dried oregano, crushed**
- **1 teaspoon sugar**
- **1/4 teaspoon salt**
- **Hot cooked noodles (optional)**
- **Yellow or green sweet pepper strips (optional)**

1

In a shallow dish stir together the flour, garlic salt, cumin, and ground red pepper. Coat steaks with flour mixture, shaking off any excess. Coat an unheated 12-inch skillet with nonstick cooking spray. Preheat over medium-high heat. Add steaks and cook for 8 to 12 minutes or until done. (Reduce heat as necessary to prevent burning while steaks cook.)

2

Meanwhile, in a medium saucepan combine undrained tomatoes, chile peppers, tomato paste, oregano, sugar, and salt. Bring to boiling; reduce heat. Simmer, uncovered, about 5 minutes or until of desired consistency. Serve tomato mixture over meat. If desired, serve with hot cooked noodles and top with sweet pepper strips.

Nutrition Facts per serving: 241 calories, 7 g total fat, 72 mg cholesterol, 421 mg sodium, 16 g carbohydrate, 30 g protein.

STEAK SALAD WITH BUTTERMILK DRESSING

If you don't have buttermilk, substitute sour milk. Just add 1 teaspoon lemon juice to a 1-cup glass measure and add enough fat-free milk to measure 1/3 cup liquid. *(Pictured on page 9.)*

Start to Finish: 35 minutes **Makes:** 4 servings

- **1 recipe Buttermilk Dressing**
- **1 cup cherry or baby pear-shape tomatoes**
- **8 cups torn mixed salad greens**
- **2 medium carrots, cut into thin, bite-size strips**
- **1 medium yellow sweet pepper, cut into thin, bite-size strips**
- **8 ounces boneless beef top sirloin steak**
- **Nonstick cooking spray**
- **1/4 cup finely shredded fresh basil**
- **Salt**
- **Ground black pepper**

1

Prepare Buttermilk Dressing. If desired, set aside a few tomatoes for garnish. Halve remaining tomatoes. Arrange salad greens, carrots, sweet pepper, and halved tomatoes in 4 salad bowls or on 4 dinner plates. Set aside. Trim fat from steak. Cut steak across the grain into thin, bite-size strips.

2

Lightly coat an unheated large skillet with nonstick cooking spray. Heat over medium-high heat. Cook and stir steak strips in hot skillet for 2 to 3 minutes or until meat is cooked through. Remove skillet from heat. Stir in basil. Lightly sprinkle with salt and black pepper to taste.

3

To serve, spoon the warm meat mixture over greens mixture. Drizzle with Buttermilk Dressing. If desired, garnish with reserved tomatoes.

Buttermilk Dressing: In a small bowl combine 1/2 cup plain low-fat yogurt; 1/3 cup buttermilk; 3 tablespoons freshly grated Parmesan cheese; 3 tablespoons finely chopped red onion; 3 tablespoons light mayonnaise dressing or salad dressing; 2 tablespoons snipped fresh parsley; 1 tablespoon white wine vinegar or lemon juice; 1 clove garlic, minced; 1/4 teaspoon salt; and 1/8 teaspoon ground black pepper. Cover and refrigerate for at least 20 minutes or until ready to serve.

Nutrition Facts per serving: 226 calories, 10 g total fat, 32 mg cholesterol, 387 mg sodium, 17 g carbohydrate, 19 g protein.

HOT AND SOUR THAI BEEF SALAD

What makes this salad Thai? Seasonings such as ginger, basil, mint, and a fiery jalapeño pepper.

Start to Finish: 30 minutes **Makes:** 4 servings

- 1 large yellow, red, or green sweet pepper, cut into thin, bite-size strips
- 1/2 of a medium cucumber, cut into thin, bite-size strips (1 cup)
- 1/4 cup lime juice
- 3 tablespoons reduced-sodium soy sauce
- 2 tablespoons brown sugar
- 1 tablespoon grated fresh ginger or 1/2 teaspoon ground ginger
- 1 tablespoon snipped fresh basil or 1 teaspoon dried basil, crushed
- 1 1/2 teaspoons snipped fresh mint or 1 teaspoon dried mint, crushed
- 12 ounces beef top sirloin steak
- Nonstick cooking spray
- 1 clove garlic, minced
- 1 fresh jalapeño pepper,* seeded and finely chopped
- 4 cups packaged torn mixed salad greens

1

In a medium bowl combine sweet pepper and cucumber. For dressing, in a small bowl stir together lime juice, soy sauce, brown sugar, ground ginger (if using), basil, and mint. Set aside.

2

Trim fat from steak. Cut into thin, bite-size strips. Coat an unheated wok or large skillet with nonstick cooking spray. Heat over medium heat. Add garlic, jalapeño pepper, and fresh ginger (if using). Stir-fry for 30 seconds. Add steak strips; stir-fry for 3 to 4 minutes or until desired doneness. Remove steak mixture from wok. Add to sweet pepper mixture. Toss gently. Add dressing to wok. Bring to boiling; boil for 30 seconds. Remove from heat.

3

To serve, divide greens among 4 dinner plates. Spoon steak mixture over greens. Drizzle with dressing.

Nutrition Facts per serving: 219 calories, 8 g total fat, 57 mg cholesterol, 468 mg sodium, 15 g carbohydrate, 22 g protein.

***Note:** Because chile peppers, such as jalapeños, contain volatile oils that can burn your skin and eyes, avoid direct contact with them as much as possible. When working with chile peppers, wear plastic or rubber gloves. If your bare hands do touch the chile peppers, wash your hands and nails well with soap and water.

GARLIC-MUSTARD STEAK SANDWICHES

It only takes minutes to put together this spunky steak strip sandwich.

Prep: 10 minutes **Broil:** 15 minutes **Makes:** 4 to 6 servings

- **2 tablespoons Dijon-style mustard**
- **1/2 teaspoon dried marjoram or thyme, crushed**
- **1/2 teaspoon bottled minced garlic or 1 clove garlic, minced**
- **1/4 teaspoon coarsely ground black pepper**
- **1 to 1 1/2 pounds beef flank steak**
- **4 to 6 hoagie rolls, split**
- **Dijon-style mustard (optional)**

1

In a small bowl combine the 2 tablespoons mustard, the marjoram or thyme, garlic, and pepper. Trim fat from steak. Brush both sides of steak with mustard mixture.

2

Place the steak on the unheated rack of a broiler pan. Broil 3 to 4 inches from the heat for 15 to 18 minutes or until medium doneness (160°), turning once halfway through broiling.

3

To serve, thinly slice steak diagonally across the grain. Spoon steak strips into hoagie rolls. If desired, pass additional mustard.

Nutrition Facts per serving: 176 calories, 9 g total fat, 53 mg cholesterol, 255 mg sodium, 1 g carbohydrate, 22 g protein.

ROAST BEEF PITAWICHES

Try these beef-stuffed pitas for lunch. Wrap each filled pita half in plastic wrap, and then chill overnight. Carry the pitawiches to work or school, keeping them well chilled in an insulated cooler.

Start to Finish: 20 minutes **Makes:** 4 servings

- **8 dried tomatoes (not oil packed)**
- **$1\frac{1}{2}$ cups packaged shredded cabbage with carrot (coleslaw mix)**
- **3 tablespoons fat-free mayonnaise dressing or salad dressing**
- **1 tablespoon fat-free milk**
- **1 teaspoon horseradish mustard**
- **$\frac{1}{4}$ teaspoon caraway seeds**
- **6 ounces thinly sliced, cooked lean roast beef**
- **2 whole wheat or white pita bread rounds, halved crosswise**

1

In a small bowl cover tomatoes with boiling water; let stand about 10 minutes or until softened. Drain tomatoes and cut into thin strips. Toss tomato strips with shredded cabbage and carrot mixture.

2

In a small bowl combine mayonnaise dressing or salad dressing, milk, mustard, and caraway seeds. Add to cabbage-tomato mixture; toss to coat.

3

To assemble sandwiches, place one-fourth of the roast beef and one-fourth of the cabbage mixture in each pita bread half.

Nutrition Facts per serving: 219 calories, 7 g total fat, 34 mg cholesterol, 434 mg sodium, 24 g carbohydrate, 16 g protein.

FESTIVE TACO BURGERS

Wrapping Tex-Mex burgers in tortillas helps corral all of the meat and toppings for easy eating.

Prep: 20 minutes **Broil:** 10 minutes **Makes:** 5 servings

- 1 cup finely chopped tomato
- 1/4 cup green or red taco sauce
- 2 tablespoons snipped fresh cilantro
- 5 7-inch flour tortillas
- 1 4-ounce can diced green chile peppers, drained
- 1/4 cup fine dry bread crumbs
- 1/4 cup finely chopped green onions
- 2 tablespoons fat-free milk
- 1 teaspoon dried oregano, crushed
- 1/2 teaspoon ground cumin
- 1/4 teaspoon ground black pepper
- 1/8 teaspoon salt
- 1 pound extra-lean ground beef
- Nonstick cooking spray
- 1 cup shredded lettuce or red cabbage
- Salsa (optional)
- Snipped fresh cilantro (optional)

1

In a medium bowl stir together tomato, taco sauce, and the 2 tablespoons cilantro. Cover and set aside. Wrap tortillas in foil; heat in a 350°F oven for 15 minutes. Remove from oven, but do not open foil packet.

2

Meanwhile, in a large bowl combine chile peppers, bread crumbs, green onions, milk, oregano, cumin, black pepper, and salt. Add meat and mix well. Shape mixture into 5 oval patties, each 4 1/2 to 5 inches long.

3

Coat the unheated rack of a broiler pan with nonstick cooking spray. Arrange patties on broiler pan. Broil 3 to 4 inches from the heat for 10 to 14 minutes or until done (160°),* turning once halfway through broiling.

4

To serve, place some of the shredded lettuce or cabbage and a patty on each tortilla; spoon some of the tomato mixture over each patty. Wrap tortillas around patties. If desired, serve with salsa and additional snipped cilantro.

Nutrition Facts per serving: 303 calories, 12 g total fat, 57 mg cholesterol, 456 mg sodium, 27 g carbohydrate, 21 g protein.

***Note:** The internal color of a ground meat patty is not a reliable doneness indicator. A beef patty cooked to 160°, regardless of color, is safe. Use an instant-read thermometer to check the internal temperature. To measure the doneness of a patty, insert an instant-read thermometer through the side of the patty to a depth of 2 to 3 inches.

BEEF AND BEAN BURRITOS

If you prefer kidney beans, use them in place of the black beans.

Start to Finish: 25 minutes **Makes:** 4 servings

- **1 recipe Quick-to-Fix Spanish Rice (optional)**
- **4 10-inch flour tortillas**
- **8 ounces lean ground beef**
- **1 cup chopped onion**
- **1 15-ounce can reduced-sodium black beans, rinsed and drained**
- **1 10-ounce can chopped tomatoes and green chile peppers**
- **1 to 2 teaspoons chili powder**
- **2 tablespoons chopped green onion**

1

If desired, prepare Quick-to-Fix Spanish Rice. Wrap tortillas in foil. Heat in a 350°F oven for 10 minutes to soften. Meanwhile, for filling, in a large skillet cook ground beef and chopped onion until meat is brown and onion is tender. Drain off fat. Stir in beans, undrained tomatoes and chile peppers, and chili powder. Bring to boiling; reduce heat. Simmer, uncovered, about 5 minutes or until desired consistency. Set aside 1/4 cup filling.

2

For each burrito, spoon one-fourth of the remaining filling onto each tortilla just below center. Fold side of tortilla opposite filling over filling. Fold in the remaining sides of tortilla just until they meet; roll up. Top burritos with the reserved filling. Sprinkle with green onion. If desired, serve with Quick-to-Fix Spanish Rice.

Nutrition Facts per serving: 321 calories, 9 g total fat, 36 mg cholesterol, 597 mg sodium, 41 g carbohydrate, 19 g protein.

Quick-to-Fix Spanish Rice: Prepare 2 cups hot cooked rice. Stir in 1 cup chopped tomato and one 4-ounce can diced green chile peppers, drained; heat through. Makes 4 servings.

ITALIAN VEAL STEW WITH POLENTA

The secret to preparing this stew in 30 minutes is cutting the veal in strips so it cooks quickly.

Start to Finish: 30 minutes **Makes:** 4 servings

- Nonstick cooking spray
- 1 medium onion, cut into wedges
- 1 medium green sweet pepper, coarsely chopped
- 2 cloves garlic, minced
- 1 14½-ounce can low-sodium tomatoes, cut up
- ¼ cup dry red wine
- 1 teaspoon instant chicken bouillon granules
- 1 teaspoon dried Italian seasoning, crushed
- 12 ounces boneless veal round steak, cut ½ inch thick
- 2¾ cups water
- ⅛ teaspoon salt
- ¾ cup quick-cooking polenta mix
- 2 cups torn fresh spinach
- Fresh parsley sprigs (optional)

1

Coat an unheated large saucepan with nonstick cooking spray. Preheat over medium heat. Cook onion, sweet pepper, and garlic in hot saucepan for 4 to 5 minutes or until vegetables are just tender, stirring occasionally. Add undrained tomatoes, wine, bouillon granules, and Italian seasoning. Bring to boiling; reduce heat. Cover and simmer for 10 minutes.

2

Meanwhile, trim fat from veal. Cut veal into bite-size strips. Coat an unheated large nonstick skillet with nonstick cooking spray. Preheat over medium heat. Stir-fry veal strips in hot skillet about 4 minutes or until cooked through.

3

In a 2-quart saucepan heat the water and salt to boiling. Stir in polenta mix. Cook, stirring frequently, for 5 minutes.

4

Add veal and spinach to tomato mixture; heat through. To serve, spoon polenta into shallow soup plates or bowls. Top with veal mixture. If desired, garnish with parsley sprigs.

Nutrition Facts per serving: 263 calories, 4 g total fat, 69 mg cholesterol, 387 mg sodium, 30 g carbohydrate, 23 g protein.

VEAL WITH APPLE-MARSALA SAUCE

If the veal you find in the supermarket is labeled "scaloppine," it is probably about 1/8 inch thick, so it will need little, if any, pounding.

Start to Finish: 25 minutes **Makes:** 4 servings

- **12 ounces veal scaloppine or boneless veal leg round steak or beef top round steak, cut 1/4 inch thick**
- **Nonstick cooking spray**
- **1 apple, thinly sliced**
- **1 clove garlic, minced**
- **1/2 cup dry Marsala**
- **1/3 cup reduced-sodium chicken broth**
- **1 tablespoon snipped fresh parsley**

1

Trim fat from veal or beef. If using veal leg round steak or beef top round steak, cut steak into 8 pieces. Place each veal piece between 2 pieces of plastic wrap. Using the flat side of a meat mallet, pound each piece to 1/8-inch thickness, working from center to edges. Remove plastic wrap.

2

Coat an unheated large skillet with nonstick cooking spray. Heat over medium-high heat. Cook half of the veal or beef in hot skillet for 2 to 4 minutes or until cooked through, turning once halfway through cooking. Transfer to a serving platter. Cover to keep warm. Repeat with remaining veal or beef.

3

Add apple and garlic to skillet. Stir in Marsala and broth. Bring to boiling; reduce heat. Boil gently, uncovered, for 4 to 5 minutes or until mixture is reduced by half.

4

To serve, spoon apple mixture over veal or beef. Sprinkle with parsley.

Nutrition Facts per serving: 167 calories, 4 g total fat, 69 mg cholesterol, 100 mg sodium, 7 g carbohydrate, 19 g protein.

MOLASSES-GLAZED PORK TENDERLOIN

Whip up some corn bread to go along with this Southern-style pork and lima bean combo.

Start to Finish: 30 minutes **Makes:** 4 servings

- **1/4 cup chopped prosciutto or 2 slices bacon, coarsely chopped**
- **1 16-ounce package frozen lima beans or two 9-ounce packages frozen Italian green beans**
- **1 medium onion, halved and thinly sliced**
- **3/4 cup water**
- **12 ounces pork tenderloin**
- **1 tablespoon olive oil**
- **1/2 cup orange juice**
- **3 tablespoons molasses**
- **1 teaspoon cornstarch**
- **1/2 teaspoon salt**
- **1/4 teaspoon ground black pepper**
- **Steamed fresh spinach or turnip greens (optional)**
- **2 tablespoons snipped fresh parsley**

1

In a large skillet cook prosciutto or bacon over medium heat until crisp-cooked; drain and set aside. In the same skillet cook beans and onion in the water according to bean package directions. Drain beans; set aside.

2

Trim fat from pork. Cut pork crosswise into 12 slices, each about 1/2 inch thick. Add oil to the same skillet; cook pork in hot oil over medium-high heat for 6 to 8 minutes or until juices run clear (160°), turning once halfway through cooking.

3

Meanwhile, in a small bowl stir together orange juice, molasses, cornstarch, salt, and pepper. Add to pork in skillet. Cook and stir until thickened and bubbly. Cook and stir 2 minutes more. Stir beans into skillet mixture; heat through.

4

To serve, if desired, divide steamed spinach among 4 dinner plates and spoon pork mixture on top. Top pork mixture with the prosciutto or bacon; sprinkle with parsley.

Nutrition Facts per serving: 324 calories, 6 g total fat, 52 mg cholesterol, 460 mg sodium, 38 g carbohydrate, 29 g protein.

PORK MEDALLIONS WITH CHERRY SAUCE

Although pork is often prepared with winter fruits, such as apples and pears, this quick-seared tenderloin shows off summertime cherries.

Start to Finish: 20 minutes **Makes:** 4 servings

- **1 cup fresh sweet cherries (such as Rainier or Bing), halved and pitted, or 1 cup frozen unsweetened pitted dark sweet cherries**
- **1 pound pork tenderloin**
- **Salt**
- **Ground black pepper**
- **Nonstick cooking spray**
- **3/4 cup cranberry juice or apple juice**
- **2 teaspoons spicy brown mustard**
- **1 teaspoon cornstarch**

1

Thaw cherries, if frozen. Trim fat from pork. Cut pork crosswise into 1-inch slices. Place each pork slice between 2 pieces of plastic wrap. Using the flat side of a meat mallet, lightly pound pork to 1/2-inch thickness, working from center to edges. Remove plastic wrap. Sprinkle lightly with salt and pepper.

2

Coat an unheated large nonstick skillet with nonstick cooking spray. Heat skillet over medium-high heat. Cook pork in hot skillet for 6 to 8 minutes or until juices run clear (160°), turning once halfway through cooking. Transfer to a serving platter; cover to keep warm.

3

In a bowl combine cranberry juice, mustard, and cornstarch; add to skillet. Cook and stir until thickened and bubbly. Cook and stir for 2 minutes more. Stir cherries into mixture in skillet.

4

To serve, spoon cherry mixture over pork.

Nutrition Facts per serving: 197 calories, 5 g total fat, 81 mg cholesterol, 127 mg sodium, 12 g carbohydrate, 26 g protein.

PEACH-SAUCED PORK

Canned peaches and quick-cooking pork tenderloin help you get a hearty meal on the table in almost no time. Serve the pork with rice and steamed broccoli.

Start to Finish: 30 minutes **Makes:** 4 servings

- **12 ounces pork tenderloin**
- **Nonstick cooking spray**
- **1 16-ounce can peach slices in light syrup**
- **1/4 cup cold water**
- **1 1/2 teaspoons cornstarch**
- **1/4 teaspoon salt**
- **1/8 teaspoon ground allspice**
- **Hot cooked rice (optional)**
- **Snipped fresh parsley (optional)**
- **Lemon peel strips (optional)**

1

Trim fat from pork. Cut pork crosswise into 16 slices, each about 1/2 inch thick. Place each pork slice between 2 pieces of plastic wrap. Using the flat side of a meat mallet, lightly pound pork to 1/4-inch thickness, working from center to edges. Remove plastic wrap.

2

Coat an unheated large skillet with nonstick cooking spray. Heat skillet over medium heat. Cook half of the pork in hot skillet for 4 to 6 minutes or until tender and juices run clear, turning once halfway through cooking. Remove pork from skillet; cover to keep warm. Repeat with remaining pork. Carefully wipe skillet with a paper towel.

3

Meanwhile, drain peaches, reserving 1/2 cup syrup. Set peaches aside. In a small bowl stir together the reserved syrup, the water, cornstarch, salt, and allspice. Add syrup mixture to skillet. Cook and stir until thickened and bubbly. Cook and stir for 2 minutes more. Add the pork and peaches to skillet; heat through.

4

To serve, if desired, arrange pork and peaches over hot cooked rice. If desired, sprinkle with parsley and garnish with lemon peel.

Nutrition Facts per serving: 174 calories, 3 g total fat, 60 mg cholesterol, 183 mg sodium, 17 g carbohydrate, 19 g protein.

PORK WITH APPLE-SOUR CREAM SAUCE

Apple slices and apple juice enhance the creamy sauce with a hint of sweetness.

Start to Finish: 30 minutes **Makes:** 4 servings

- **1 9-ounce package refrigerated spinach fettuccine or 4 ounces dried spinach fettuccine**
- **12 ounces pork tenderloin**
- **Nonstick cooking spray**
- **1 medium apple, cored and thinly sliced**
- **3/4 cup apple juice or apple cider**
- **1 small onion, chopped**
- **1/4 teaspoon salt**
- **1/4 teaspoon dried sage, crushed**
- **1 8-ounce carton fat-free dairy sour cream**
- **2 tablespoons all-purpose flour**
- **Cracked black pepper (optional)**

1

Cook fettuccine according to package directions. Drain fettuccine. Return to pan. Cover; keep warm. Meanwhile, trim fat from pork. Cut pork crosswise into 4 slices. Place each pork slice between 2 pieces of plastic wrap. Using the flat side of a meat mallet, lightly pound pork to 1/2-inch thickness, working from center to edges. Remove plastic wrap.

2

Coat an unheated large skillet with nonstick cooking spray. Heat the skillet over medium heat. Cook half of the pork slices in hot skillet over medium-high heat for 6 to 8 minutes or until juices run clear (160°), turning once halfway through cooking. Remove pork from skillet. Cover to keep warm. Repeat with remaining pork slices.

3

For sauce, add apple slices, apple juice or cider, onion, salt, and sage to skillet. Bring just to boiling; reduce heat. Cover and simmer for 4 to 5 minutes or until apple is just tender. Using a slotted spoon, carefully remove apple slices and set aside. In a small bowl stir together sour cream and flour. Add sour cream mixture to skillet. Cook and stir until thickened and bubbly. Cook and stir for 1 minute more.

4

To serve, arrange pork and apple slices over fettuccine. Spoon sauce over pork, apple slices, and pasta. If desired, sprinkle with pepper.

Nutrition Facts per serving: 373 calories, 4 g total fat, 60 mg cholesterol, 231 mg sodium, 54 g carbohydrate, 28 g protein.

GARLIC PORK BALSAMICO

In this low-cal entrée, a tangy honey-mustard sauce combines with the mellow flavor of roasted garlic to enhance the tender pork slices.

Start to Finish: 30 minutes **Makes:** 4 servings

1 small bulb garlic (about 10 cloves)
1 cup water
12 ounces boneless pork loin
1 teaspoon dried rosemary, crushed
1 teaspoon olive oil
1/4 cup balsamic vinegar
2 tablespoons water
2 tablespoons honey mustard

1

Separate garlic bulb into cloves. Do not peel. In a small saucepan combine garlic cloves and the 1 cup water. Bring to boiling. Boil for 2 minutes. Drain; cool slightly. Peel cloves and set aside.

2

Trim fat from pork. Cut pork into 3/4-inch slices. Sprinkle both sides of each pork slice with dried rosemary, pressing into surface of the pork.

3

In a large nonstick skillet heat oil. Cook pork and garlic cloves over medium heat for 8 to 12 minutes or until juices run clear (160°), turning once halfway through cooking. Remove the pork, leaving the garlic cloves in the skillet. Cover the pork to keep warm.

4

For sauce, stir together vinegar, the 2 tablespoons water, and the honey mustard. Add to garlic in skillet, stirring to scrape up any browned bits. Bring mixture just to boiling; reduce heat. Simmer for 1 to 2 minutes or until sauce becomes slightly thickened.

5

To serve, spoon sauce over pork.

Nutrition Facts per serving: 143 calories, 7 g total fat, 38 mg cholesterol, 128 mg sodium, 6 g carbohydrate, 13 g protein.

APRICOT PORK MEDALLIONS

Apricots and plum jam team up for a sweet-tart sauce that complements the delicate pork.

Start to Finish: 20 minutes **Makes:** 4 servings

1 cup quick-cooking rice
12 ounces pork tenderloin
1 tablespoon margarine or butter
1 16-ounce can unpeeled apricot halves in light syrup
1 tablespoon cornstarch
1/4 cup red plum jam or currant jelly
2 tablespoons white wine vinegar
2 green onions, sliced

1

In a medium saucepan cook rice according to package directions. Meanwhile, trim fat from pork. Cut pork into 3/4-inch slices. Place each pork slice between 2 sheets of plastic wrap. Using the flat side of a meat mallet, pound pork to 1/2-inch thickness, working from center to edges. Remove plastic wrap.

2

In a large skillet cook pork in hot margarine or butter over medium-high heat for 4 to 8 minutes or until juices run clear, turning once halfway through cooking. Remove pork from skillet. Cover to keep warm.

3

Meanwhile, for sauce, drain apricots, reserving 2/3 cup of the syrup. Set syrup aside. Slice apricots. In a small saucepan stir together the reserved apricot syrup and the cornstarch. Stir in plum jam or currant jelly and vinegar. Cook and stir over medium heat until thickened and bubbly. Cook and stir for 2 minutes more. Stir in apricots. Heat through.

4

To serve, divide rice among 4 dinner plates. Top with pork. Spoon sauce over pork. Sprinkle with sliced green onions.

Nutrition Facts per serving: 341 calories, 6 g total fat, 60 mg cholesterol, 85 mg sodium, 50 g carbohydrate, 21 g protein.

PORK CHOPS SMOTHERED WITH PEPPERS AND ONION

This pork version of pepper steak is loaded with colorful sweet peppers and onion.

Start to Finish: 25 minutes **Makes:** 4 servings

- **4 pork loin or pork rib chops, cut 1/2 to 3/4 inch thick (about 1 1/4 pounds total)**
- **1 tablespoon olive oil**
- **1 red sweet pepper, cut into thin, bite-size strips**
- **1 green sweet pepper, cut into thin, bite-size strips**
- **1 yellow sweet pepper, cut into thin, bite-size strips**
- **1 large sweet onion, thinly sliced**
- **1/4 cup water**
- **1/4 cup dry white wine or chicken broth**
- **1 teaspoon snipped fresh rosemary or 1/2 teaspoon dried rosemary, crushed**
- **1/4 teaspoon salt**
- **4 slices crusty bread**

1

Trim fat from chops. In a large skillet heat oil. Cook chops in hot oil over medium-high heat for 4 to 5 minutes or until browned, turning to brown evenly. Remove chops from skillet; set aside. Add sweet peppers and onion to skillet. Cook, stirring frequently, about 10 minutes or until vegetables are tender.

2

Return chops to skillet; add the water, wine or broth, rosemary, and salt. Bring to boiling; reduce heat. Cover and simmer for 5 to 6 minutes or until juices run clear (160°).

3

To serve, spoon vegetables over chops. Serve with bread.

Nutrition Facts per serving: 273 calories, 12 g total fat, 51 mg cholesterol, 328 mg sodium, 20 g carbohydrate, 19 g protein.

SOUTHWEST PORK CHOPS WITH CORN SALSA

Cilantro and jalapeño pepper give these succulent chops a Southwestern flavor.

Prep: 20 minutes **Grill:** 11 minutes **Makes:** 4 servings

- **1 cup fresh or frozen whole kernel corn**
- **3 tablespoons white wine vinegar**
- **1 tablespoon snipped fresh cilantro**
- **1 teaspoon olive oil**
- **3 plum tomatoes, chopped**
- **1/2 cup thinly sliced green onions**
- **1 small fresh jalapeño pepper,* seeded and finely chopped**
- **2 tablespoons snipped fresh cilantro**
- **1 tablespoon white wine vinegar**
- **4 center-cut pork loin chops, cut 3/4 inch thick**
- **Cactus leaves (optional)**
- **Fresh cilantro sprigs (optional)**

1

Thaw corn, if frozen. For sauce, in a small bowl combine the 3 tablespoons vinegar, the 1 tablespoon snipped cilantro, and the oil. Set aside.

2

For corn salsa, in a covered small saucepan cook fresh corn (if using) in a small amount of boiling water for 2 to 3 minutes or until corn is crisp-tender; drain. In a medium bowl combine the corn, tomatoes, green onions, jalapeño pepper, the 2 tablespoons snipped cilantro, and the 1 tablespoon vinegar. Set aside.

3

Trim fat from chops. Grill chops on the rack of an uncovered grill directly over medium coals for 11 to 14 minutes or until juices run clear (160°), turning once halfway through grilling and brushing occasionally with sauce up to the last 5 minutes of grilling.

4

To serve, if desired, arrange chops on cactus leaves and garnish with cilantro sprigs. Serve with the corn salsa.

Nutrition Facts per serving: 201 calories, 9 g total fat, 51 mg cholesterol, 51 mg sodium, 14 g carbohydrate, 18 g protein.

***Note:** Because chile peppers, such as jalapeños, contain volatile oils that can burn your skin and eyes, avoid direct contact with them as much as possible. When working with chile peppers, wear plastic or rubber gloves. If your bare hands do touch the chile peppers, wash your hands and nails well with soap and water.

SPICED PEAR AND PORK CHOPS

No pumpkin pie spice? Use 1/8 teaspoon each ground ginger, cinnamon, nutmeg, and cloves.

Prep: 20 minutes **Broil:** 8 minutes **Makes:** 4 servings

- **1 cup pear nectar or white grape juice**
- **1/2 cup coarsely chopped onion**
- **1 teaspoon instant chicken bouillon granules**
- **1/2 teaspoon pumpkin pie spice**
- **2 medium pears, cored and sliced**
- **4 pork loin chops, cut 1/2 inch thick (about 1 1/4 pounds total)**

1

In a medium saucepan combine pear nectar or white grape juice, onion, bouillon granules, and pumpkin pie spice. Bring to boiling. Add pear slices. Return to boiling; reduce heat. Cover and simmer for 3 to 4 minutes or until crisp-tender. Using a slotted spoon, remove pear slices and onion from the saucepan. Cover to keep warm.

2

Gently boil juice mixture in saucepan, uncovered, for 3 to 5 minutes or until reduced to 1/2 cup.

3

Meanwhile, trim fat from chops. Place chops on the unheated rack of a broiler pan. Broil 3 to 4 inches from the heat for 4 minutes. Brush with some of the juice mixture. Turn and broil 4 to 7 minutes more or until juices run clear (160°). Brush again with some of the juice mixture.

4

To serve, top chops with pear and onion mixture. Drizzle with any remaining juice mixture.

Nutrition Facts per serving: 223 calories, 8 g total fat, 48 mg cholesterol, 256 mg sodium, 24 g carbohydrate, 15 g protein.

SHERRIED PORK

Team these easy pork cutlets with steamed baby carrots and peas.

Start to Finish: 25 minutes **Makes:** 4 servings

12 ounces pork tenderloin
1 beaten egg
1 tablespoon milk
½ cup cornflake crumbs
⅛ teaspoon garlic powder
2 tablespoons margarine or butter
¼ cup water
¼ cup dry sherry, dry Marsala, or water
1 teaspoon instant chicken bouillon granules
Dash ground black pepper
1 tablespoon snipped fresh parsley

1

Trim fat from pork. Cut crosswise into 4 slices. Place each slice between two pieces of plastic wrap. Using the flat side of a meat mallet, pound pork to ¼-inch thickness, working from center to edges. Remove plastic wrap. In a shallow bowl combine egg and milk. In another bowl combine cornflake crumbs and garlic powder. Dip each pork slice into the egg mixture. Dip into the crumb mixture, coating well.

2

In a large skillet cook pork slices in the hot margarine or butter for 4 to 8 minutes or until juices run clear, turning once halfway through cooking. Remove from skillet. Keep warm.

3

Stir the ¼ cup water; the ¼ cup sherry, Marsala, or water; bouillon granules; and pepper into the drippings in the skillet, scraping up any browned bits. Bring to boiling. Boil rapidly for 2 to 3 minutes or until mixture thickens slightly. Serve over pork slices. Sprinkle with parsley.

Nutrition Facts per serving: 224 calories, 10 g total fat, 114 mg cholesterol, 416 mg sodium, 7 g carbohydrate, 21 g protein.

CUMBERLAND PORK MEDALLIONS

If you like, use apple juice in place of the wine for a nonalcoholic version of these ruby-sauced slices.

Start to Finish: 25 minutes **Makes:** 4 servings

- **1 pound pork tenderloin**
- **1 tablespoon cooking oil or olive oil**
- **1/4 cup sliced green onions**
- **1/2 cup dry red or white wine or apple juice**
- **1/2 cup chicken broth**
- **2 tablespoons currant jelly**
- **1 teaspoon Dijon-style mustard**
- **1 tablespoon chicken broth or cold water**
- **1 teaspoon cornstarch**

1

Trim fat from pork. Cut crosswise into 3/4-inch slices. In a 10-inch skillet heat oil over medium heat. Cook pork about 8 minutes or until juices run clear (160°), turning once halfway through cooking. Remove meat from skillet; keep warm.

2

Add green onions to skillet; cook just until tender. Carefully add wine or apple juice and the 1/2 cup broth. Boil gently over medium-high heat about 4 minutes or until reduced to about 1/2 cup. Add jelly and mustard, stirring until jelly is melted. Combine the 1 tablespoon broth or cold water and the cornstarch; stir into skillet. Cook and stir over medium heat until thickened and bubbly. Cook and stir for 1 minute more. Serve sauce with the pork medallions.

Nutrition Facts per serving: 231 calories, 8 g total fat, 81 mg cholesterol, 220 mg sodium, 8 g carbohydrate, 26 g protein.

JAMAICAN PORK AND SWEET POTATO STIR-FRY

The jerk seasoning gives the pork strips tropical-island flair.

Start to Finish: 20 minutes **Makes:** 4 servings

1½ cups quick-cooking rice
¼ cup thinly sliced green onions
1 large sweet potato (about 12 ounces)
1 medium tart apple (such as Granny Smith), cored
12 ounces lean boneless pork strips for stir-frying
2 to 3 teaspoons Jamaican jerk seasoning
1 tablespoon cooking oil
⅓ cup apple juice or water

1

Prepare rice according to package directions. Stir half of the green onions into cooked rice. Meanwhile, peel sweet potato. Cut into quarters lengthwise; thinly slice crosswise. Place in a microwave-safe pie plate or shallow dish. Cover with vented plastic wrap. Microwave on 100-percent power (high) for 3 to 4 minutes or until tender, stirring once halfway through cooking. Cut apple into 16 wedges. Sprinkle pork strips with Jamaican jerk seasoning; toss to coat evenly.

2

Pour oil into a wok or large skillet. (Add more oil, if necessary, during cooking.) Heat over medium-high heat. Stir-fry seasoned pork in hot oil for 2 minutes. Add apple and remaining green onions; stir-fry for 1 to 2 minutes or until pork is cooked through. Stir in sweet potato and apple juice. Bring to boiling; reduce heat. Simmer, uncovered, for 1 minute more.

3

To serve, divide pork and rice mixtures among 4 soup bowls or dinner plates.

Nutrition Facts per serving: 365 calories, 9 g total fat, 38 mg cholesterol, 131 mg sodium, 54 g carbohydrate, 16 g protein.

BALSAMIC PORK AND BERRY SALAD

When you're in a hurry, slice the romaine rather than tearing it.

Start to Finish: 30 minutes **Makes:** 4 servings

8 cups torn romaine
2 cups sliced fresh strawberries
1/2 cup thinly sliced celery
8 ounces pork tenderloin
Nonstick cooking spray
1 teaspoon olive oil or salad oil
1 teaspoon bottled minced garlic
1/4 cup honey
1/4 cup balsamic vinegar
1/4 teaspoon ground black pepper
2 tablespoons chopped pecans or walnuts, toasted
1 teaspoon snipped fresh chives

1

In a large bowl toss together romaine, strawberries, and celery. Set aside.

2

Trim fat from pork. Cut pork crosswise into 1/4-inch slices. Coat an unheated large skillet with nonstick cooking spray. Heat over medium-high heat. Cook pork, half at a time, in hot skillet for about 4 minutes or until juices run clear, turning once halfway through cooking. Remove pork from skillet. Cover to keep warm.

3

For dressing, add oil to skillet. Cook and stir garlic in hot oil for 15 seconds. Stir in honey, vinegar, and pepper. Cook and stir until heated through.

4

To serve, arrange romaine mixture on 4 dinner plates. Top with the pork. Drizzle with dressing. Sprinkle with nuts and chives.

Nutrition Facts per serving: 227 calories, 6 g total fat, 40 mg cholesterol, 54 mg sodium, 30 g carbohydrate, 15 g protein.

BLACK BEANS AND RICE WITH MANGO

Look for spicy chorizo at Mexican food stores, or substitute hot Italian sausage.

Start to Finish: 20 minutes **Makes:** 4 servings

- 1/2 cup chopped red sweet pepper
- 1/2 cup chopped onion
- 1/4 cup crumbled uncooked chorizo sausage
- 3 cloves garlic, minced
- 1 15-ounce can black beans, rinsed and drained
- 3/4 cup water
- 1 teaspoon dried oregano, crushed
- 1/4 crushed red pepper
- Salt
- 2 cups hot cooked rice
- 1/2 cup chopped fresh mango
- Fresh oregano sprigs (optional)

1

In a large skillet cook sweet pepper, onion, chorizo, and garlic over medium-high heat for 4 to 5 minutes or until sausage is browned. Add beans, the water, oregano, and crushed red pepper. Bring to boiling; reduce heat. Cover and simmer for 10 minutes. Season to taste with salt.

2

To serve, spoon bean mixture over rice. Top with mango. If desired, garnish with oregano sprigs.

Nutrition Facts per serving: 201 calories, 5 g total fat, 0 mg cholesterol, 400 mg sodium, 44 g carbohydrate, 12 g protein.

GROUND PORK PATTIES WITH HERBED SWEET POTATO CHIPS

Homemade baked sweet potato chips are a delicious addition to this sensational supper.

Start to Finish: 35 minutes **Makes:** 4 servings

- **1 recipe Herbed Sweet Potato Chips**
- **12 ounces lean ground pork**
- **2 green onions, finely chopped**
- **1/4 teaspoon seasoned salt**
- **1/4 teaspoon ground black pepper**
- **1/2 cup apple juice or apple cider**
- **2 tablespoons coarse-grain brown mustard**
- **1 tablespoon brown sugar**
- **1 teaspoon cornstarch**
- **1/2 teaspoon dried sage, crushed**
- **3 cups shredded lettuce**
- **Baby pear-shape tomatoes**

1

Prepare Herbed Sweet Potato Chips. In a medium bowl combine pork, green onions, seasoned salt, and pepper. Shape meat mixture into four 1/2-inch patties. In a large skillet cook patties over medium heat for 5 minutes. Turn and cook for 5 minutes more. Pour off any drippings.

2

Meanwhile, for sauce, in a small saucepan combine apple juice, mustard, brown sugar, cornstarch, and sage. Cook and stir over medium heat until thickened and bubbly. Cook and stir for 2 minutes more. Turn patties again; brush with some of the sauce. Cook for 3 to 4 minutes more or until done (160°).*

3

To serve, divide shredded lettuce among 4 dinner plates. Add a patty to each plate. Top each with about 2 tablespoons of the sauce. Garnish with tomatoes. Serve with Herbed Sweet Potato Chips.

Herbed Sweet Potato Chips: Coat a 15×10×1-inch baking pan with nonstick cooking spray; set aside. In a large bowl combine 1 pound sweet potatoes, sliced 1/8 inch thick; 1 tablespoon cooking oil; 2 teaspoons salt-free seasoning; and 1/2 teaspoon barbecue seasoning. Toss gently to coat. Spread evenly in single layer on prepared baking pan. Bake in 450°F oven for 12 to 15 minutes or until tender.

Nutrition Facts per serving: 272 calories, 11 g total fat, 40 mg cholesterol, 306 mg sodium, 31 g carbohydrate, 13 g protein.

***Note:** The internal color of a ground meat patty is not a reliable doneness indicator. A pork patty cooked to 160°, regardless of color, is safe. Use an instant-read thermometer to check the internal temperature. To measure the doneness of a patty, insert an instant-read thermometer through the side of the patty to a depth of 2 to 3 inches.

PIZZA SOUP

This quick-as-a-wink soup is not only good for your kids, it's full of the flavors they love.

Start to Finish: 20 minutes **Makes:** 6 servings

- **1 cup chopped onion**
- **1 cup chopped green sweet pepper**
- **1 cup sliced fresh mushrooms**
- **1 cup halved, sliced zucchini**
- **1 13¾-ounce can low-sodium beef-flavored broth**
- **1 14½-ounce can low-sodium tomatoes or one 14½-ounce can Italian-style tomatoes, cut up**
- **1 8-ounce can pizza sauce**
- **4 ounces cooked smoked sausage links, thinly sliced**
- **½ teaspoon pizza seasoning**
- **½ cup shredded reduced-fat mozzarella cheese (2 ounces)**

1

In a medium saucepan combine onion, sweet pepper, mushrooms, zucchini, and ¼ cup of the broth. Bring to boiling; reduce heat. Cover and simmer for 5 minutes.

2

Stir in the remaining broth, the undrained tomatoes, pizza sauce, sausage, and pizza seasoning. Simmer for 5 to 10 minutes more or until the vegetables are tender.

3

To serve, top with shredded cheese.

Nutrition Facts per serving: 167 calories, 9 g total fat, 19 mg cholesterol, 542 mg sodium, 11 g carbohydrate, 10 g protein.

HAM AND CHEESE FRITTATA

Don't be intimidated by making a frittata—it's easy. Once the egg mixture is in the pan, just run a spatula around the edge, lifting the egg mixture so the uncooked portion flows underneath.

Start to Finish: 25 minutes **Makes:** 6 servings

Nonstick cooking spray
1 cup chopped cooked ham (about 5 ounces)
1/2 cup chopped onion
1/2 cup chopped green or red sweet pepper
6 slightly beaten eggs
3/4 cup low-fat cottage cheese
1/8 teaspoon ground black pepper
2 plum tomatoes, thinly sliced
1/4 cup shredded reduced-fat cheddar cheese (1 ounce)

1

Coat an unheated 10-inch ovenproof skillet with nonstick cooking spray. Heat skillet over medium heat. Cook ham, onion, and sweet pepper in hot skillet about 4 minutes or until vegetables are tender and ham is lightly browned.

2

Meanwhile, in a medium bowl combine eggs, cottage cheese, and black pepper. Pour over ham mixture in skillet. Cook over medium-low heat. As egg mixture sets, run a spatula around the edge of the skillet, lifting egg mixture so uncooked portion flows underneath. Continue cooking and lifting edges until egg mixture is almost set but still glossy and moist.

3

Place skillet under broiler 5 inches from heat. Broil for 1 to 2 minutes or until eggs are set. Arrange tomato slices on top of frittata. Sprinkle cheese over tomato. Broil 1 minute more.

Nutrition Facts per serving: 161 calories, 8 g total fat, 231 mg cholesterol, 494 mg sodium, 5 g carbohydrate, 17 g protein.

LAMB PEPPER CHOPS

The hot cooked rice is well worth including—a $\frac{1}{2}$-cup serving adds only about 100 calories.

Start to Finish: 30 minutes **Makes:** 4 servings

- **3 tablespoons reduced-calorie orange marmalade or apricot preserves**
- **2 tablespoons hoisin sauce**
- **1 tablespoon water**
- **4 lamb leg sirloin chops, cut $\frac{3}{4}$ inch thick (about $1\frac{1}{2}$ pounds total)**
- **Nonstick cooking spray**
- **1 medium red sweet pepper, cut into thin, bite-size strips**
- **1 medium green sweet pepper, cut into thin, bite-size strips**
- **2 teaspoons cold water**
- **1 teaspoon cornstarch**
- **Hot cooked rice (optional)**

1

In a small bowl stir together orange marmalade or apricot preserves, hoisin sauce, and the 1 tablespoon water. Set aside.

2

Trim fat from chops. Coat an unheated large skillet with nonstick cooking spray. Heat over medium heat. Cook chops in hot skillet for 7 minutes. Turn and top with sweet pepper strips. Pour marmalade mixture evenly over chops and vegetables.

3

Bring mixture to boiling; reduce heat. Cover and simmer for 7 to 10 minutes or until chops are medium doneness (160°). Remove chops and pepper strips from skillet; cover to keep warm.

4

For sauce, in a small bowl stir together the 2 teaspoons cold water and the cornstarch. Add to liquid in skillet. Cook and stir until thickened and bubbly. Cook and stir for 2 minutes more.

5

To serve, if desired, arrange chops and pepper strips over rice on 4 dinner plates. Spoon sauce over chops and pepper strips.

Nutrition Facts per serving: 208 calories, 7 g total fat, 69 mg cholesterol, 212 mg sodium, 12 g carbohydrate, 22 g protein.

TUSCAN LAMB CHOP SKILLET

White kidney beans are a Tuscan favorite. Here they are flavored with rosemary and garlic.

Start to Finish: 20 minutes **Makes:** 4 servings

- **8 lamb rib chops, cut 1 inch thick (about $1^{1}/_{2}$ pounds total)**
- **2 teaspoons olive oil**
- **3 cloves garlic, minced**
- **1 19-ounce can white kidney beans (cannellini beans), rinsed and drained**
- **1 8-ounce can Italian-style stewed tomatoes**
- **1 tablespoon balsamic vinegar**
- **2 teaspoons snipped fresh rosemary**
- **Fresh rosemary sprigs (optional)**

1

Trim fat from chops. In a large skillet heat oil. Cook chops in hot oil over medium heat 9 to 11 minutes or until medium doneness (160°), turning once halfway through cooking. Transfer chops to a plate; keep warm.

2

Stir garlic into drippings in skillet. Cook and stir for 1 minute. Stir in beans, undrained tomatoes, vinegar, and snipped rosemary. Bring to boiling; reduce heat. Simmer, uncovered, for 3 minutes.

3

Spoon bean mixture onto 4 dinner plates; arrange 2 chops on each plate. If desired, garnish with rosemary sprigs.

Nutrition Facts per serving: 272 calories, 9 g total fat, 67 mg cholesterol, 466 mg sodium, 24 g carbohydrate, 30 g protein.

LAMB CHOPS WITH SWEET POTATO CHUTNEY

A made-from-scratch chutney adds an intriguing accent to these succulent chops.

Start to Finish: 30 minutes **Makes:** 4 servings

- **8 lamb rib or loin chops, cut 1 inch thick (about 1½ pounds total)**
- **⅓ cup finely chopped shallots**
- **¼ teaspoon crushed red pepper**
- **¼ cup packed brown sugar**
- **¼ cup vinegar**
- **2 tablespoons dried cranberries or currants**
- **½ teaspoon grated fresh ginger**
- **1 medium sweet potato, peeled and cubed**

1

Trim fat from chops. In a small bowl combine the shallots and crushed red pepper. Set aside 2 tablespoons of the shallot mixture. Sprinkle the remaining shallot mixture evenly over chops; rub in with your fingers. Place chops on the unheated rack of a broiler pan. Set aside.

2

For chutney, in a medium saucepan combine the 2 tablespoons shallot mixture, the brown sugar, vinegar, cranberries or currants, and ginger. Stir in sweet potato. Bring to boiling; reduce heat. Cover and simmer for 10 minutes, stirring occasionally.

3

Meanwhile, broil chops 3 to 4 inches from the heat for 10 to 15 minutes or until medium doneness (160°), turning once halfway through broiling. Serve the chops with the chutney.

Nutrition Facts per serving: 317 calories, 11 g total fat, 97 mg cholesterol, 83 mg sodium, 24 g carbohydrate, 30 g protein.

HONEY-MUSTARD LAMB CHOPS

A medley of Dijon-style mustard, honey, and rosemary brings out the best in lamb chops.

Prep: 10 minutes **Broil:** 10 minutes **Makes:** 2 servings

4 small lamb loin chops (about 12 ounces total)
2 small zucchini, halved lengthwise
1 tablespoon Dijon-style mustard
1 tablespoon honey
1½ teaspoons snipped fresh rosemary or ½ teaspoon dried rosemary, crushed

1

Trim fat from chops. Arrange chops and zucchini halves, cut sides up, on the unheated rack of a broiler pan.

2

In a small bowl stir together mustard, honey, and rosemary. Spread some of the mustard mixture on top of the chops.

3

Broil chops and zucchini 3 inches from the heat for 6 minutes. Turn chops and zucchini; spread remaining mustard mixture on chops and zucchini. Broil chops and zucchini 4 to 9 minutes more or until lamb is of medium doneness (160°) and the zucchini is tender.

Nutrition Facts per serving: 301 calories, 12 g total fat, 107 mg cholesterol, 287 mg sodium, 13 g carbohydrate, 35 g protein.

POULTRY

You'll be delighted that these chicken and turkey entrées can be so good for you and so satisfying.

Mediterranean Chicken and Pasta
(see recipe, page 117)

CHICKEN WITH CHERRY SAUCE

Because this recipe calls for dried cherries, you can make it year round. Look for them in the produce department or with other dried fruits at your supermarket.

Start to Finish: 30 minutes **Makes:** 4 servings

- **4 small skinless, boneless chicken breast halves (about 12 ounces total)**
- **Ground nutmeg**
- **1/3 cup reduced-sodium chicken broth**
- **1/3 cup unsweetened pineapple juice**
- **2 teaspoons cornstarch**
- **1 teaspoon brown sugar**
- **Dash ground black pepper**
- **1/4 cup dried tart red cherries or golden raisins, coarsely chopped**
- **Hot cooked long grain and wild rice mix (optional)**

1

Sprinkle chicken lightly with nutmeg. Place chicken, boned side up, on the unheated rack of a broiler pan. Broil 4 to 5 inches from the heat for 7 minutes. Turn chicken; broil for 5 to 8 minutes more or until chicken is tender and no longer pink.

2

Meanwhile, for sauce, in a small saucepan combine broth, pineapple juice, cornstarch, brown sugar, and pepper. Mix well. Cook and stir over medium heat until thickened and bubbly. Stir in cherries or raisins. Cook and stir for 2 minutes more.

3

To serve, spoon sauce over chicken. If desired, serve with hot cooked rice mix.

Nutrition Facts per serving: 137 calories, 2 g total fat, 45 mg cholesterol, 74 mg sodium, 11 g carbohydrate, 17 g protein.

CHICKEN IN SOUR CREAM SAUCE

Sherry adds a subtle background flavor to the sour cream sauce.

Start to Finish: 25 minutes **Makes:** 4 servings

- Nonstick cooking spray
- 4 small skinless, boneless chicken breast halves (about 12 ounces total)
- 1 teaspoon olive oil
- 2 cups sliced fresh mushrooms
- 1 cup red and/or green sweet pepper cut into 3/4-inch squares
- 1 clove garlic, minced
- 1/2 cup reduced-sodium chicken broth
- Salt
- Ground black pepper
- 1/2 cup fat-free dairy sour cream
- 1 tablespoon all-purpose flour
- 1/8 teaspoon ground black pepper
- 1 tablespoon dry sherry (optional)
- 2 cups hot cooked white or brown rice
- Snipped fresh parsley (optional)
- Whole fresh chives (optional)
- Edible flowers (optional)

1

Coat an unheated large nonstick skillet with nonstick cooking spray. Heat skillet. Cook chicken in hot skillet over medium heat about 4 minutes or until browned, turning to brown evenly. Remove chicken from skillet.

2

Carefully add oil to hot skillet. Cook mushrooms, sweet pepper, and garlic in hot oil until tender. Remove vegetables from skillet; cover with foil to keep warm. Carefully stir broth into skillet. Return chicken breasts to skillet. Sprinkle chicken lightly with salt and black pepper. Bring to boiling; reduce heat. Cover and simmer for 5 to 7 minutes or until chicken is tender and no longer pink. Transfer chicken to a serving platter; cover to keep warm.

3

For sauce, in a small bowl stir together sour cream, flour, and the 1/8 teaspoon black pepper until smooth. If desired, stir in the sherry. Stir into mixture in skillet. Cook and stir until thickened and bubbly. Cook and stir for 1 minute more.

4

To serve, spoon chicken, vegetables, and sauce over hot cooked rice. If desired, garnish with parsley, chives, and flowers.

Nutrition Facts per serving: 259 calories, 4 g total fat, 45 mg cholesterol, 176 mg sodium, 32 g carbohydrate, 22 g protein.

CHICKEN WITH GRAPES

Using both red and green grapes makes the delicate sauce more colorful.

Start to Finish: 20 minutes **Makes:** 4 servings

- **Nonstick cooking spray**
- **4 small skinless, boneless chicken breast halves (about 12 ounces total)**
- **1/2 cup white grape juice, apple juice, or apple cider**
- **1 teaspoon instant chicken bouillon granules**
- **1 teaspoon cornstarch**
- **1 cup seedless green and/or red grapes, halved**

1

Coat an unheated large skillet with nonstick cooking spray. Heat skillet over medium to medium-high heat. Cook chicken in hot skillet for 8 to 10 minutes or until chicken is tender and no longer pink, turning to brown evenly. Remove from skillet; cover to keep warm.

2

Meanwhile, in a small bowl combine grape juice, apple juice, or cider; bouillon granules; and cornstarch. Add to skillet. Cook and stir until thickened and bubbly. Cook and stir for 2 minutes more. Stir in grapes; heat through.

3

To serve, spoon grape mixture over chicken.

Nutrition Facts per serving: 143 calories, 3 g total fat, 45 mg cholesterol, 258 mg sodium, 13 g carbohydrate, 17 g protein.

BROILED CHICKEN WITH FRESH PLUM SAUCE

When looking for plums, select ones that are firm, plump, and well-shaped. Ripe plums will give slightly to gentle pressure.

Start to Finish: 25 minutes **Makes:** 4 servings

- **4 small skinless, boneless chicken breast halves (about 12 ounces total)**
- **3 medium fresh plums, pitted and sliced (1½ cups)**
- **½ cup grape juice**
- **1 teaspoon snipped fresh rosemary or ¼ teaspoon dried rosemary, crushed**
- **½ teaspoon sugar**
- **1 tablespoon cold water**
- **2 teaspoons cornstarch**
- **2 tablespoons snipped fresh parsley (optional)**
- **2 cups hot cooked rice (optional)**
- **Fresh rosemary sprigs (optional)**

1

Place chicken on the unheated rack of a broiler pan. Broil 4 to 5 inches from heat for 12 to 15 minutes or until chicken is tender and no longer pink, turning once halfway through broiling.

2

Meanwhile, for sauce, in a medium saucepan combine plums, grape juice, snipped or dried rosemary, and sugar. Bring to boiling; reduce heat. Cover and simmer for 3 minutes. In a small bowl stir together the water and cornstarch. Stir into the plum mixture. Cook and stir until thickened and bubbly. Cook and stir for 2 minutes more.

3

To serve, if desired, stir parsley into rice. Serve chicken with rice mixture and top with sauce. If desired, garnish with rosemary sprigs.

Nutrition Facts per serving: 134 calories, 2 g total fat, 45 mg cholesterol, 42 mg sodium, 11 g carbohydrate, 16 g protein.

CHICKEN WITH TOMATOES AND PEPPERS

Stewed tomatoes and three kinds of peppers make this dish as colorful as it is tasty.

Start to Finish: 30 minutes **Makes:** 6 servings

- **6 medium skinless, boneless chicken breast halves (about 1½ pounds total)**
- **¼ teaspoon salt**
- **⅛ teaspoon ground black pepper**
- **1 tablespoon margarine or butter**
- **1 8-ounce can stewed tomatoes**
- **1 small onion, chopped**
- **½ cup finely chopped red sweet pepper**
- **½ cup finely chopped green sweet pepper**
- **½ cup finely chopped yellow sweet pepper**
- **2 tablespoons dry white wine**
- **1 teaspoon chili powder**
- **¼ teaspoon ground cumin**
- **Red, green, and/or yellow sweet pepper rings (optional)**
- **3 cups hot cooked rice**

1

Sprinkle both sides of chicken with salt and black pepper. In a large skillet cook chicken in hot margarine or butter until browned on both sides, turning to brown evenly. Drain off fat. In a medium bowl combine undrained stewed tomatoes, onion, chopped sweet peppers, wine, chili powder, and cumin. Pour over chicken. Cover and simmer for 10 to 12 minutes or until chicken is tender and no longer pink. Remove chicken to a serving platter; cover to keep warm.

2

Heat the tomato mixture to boiling. Boil, uncovered, for 4 to 6 minutes or until desired consistency.

3

To serve, spoon tomato mixture over chicken. If desired, garnish with pepper rings. Serve with hot cooked rice.

Nutrition Facts per serving: 274 calories, 5 g total fat, 50 mg cholesterol, 260 mg sodium, 34 g carbohydrate, 22 g protein.

CHICKEN WITH CITRUS-LEEK SAUCE

A touch of vermouth or dry white wine complements the citrusy sauce.

Start to Finish: 25 minutes **Makes:** 4 servings

- **2 teaspoons cooking oil**
- **1 medium leek, thinly sliced (about 1/2 cup)**
- **4 small skinless, boneless chicken breast halves (about 12 ounces total)**
- **1/2 cup orange-grapefruit juice or orange juice**
- **2 tablespoons dry vermouth or dry white wine**
- **2 tablespoons reduced-calorie orange marmalade**
- **2 cups hot cooked couscous or rice (optional)**

1

In a large skillet heat oil. Cook leek in hot oil over medium heat for 2 minutes; remove from skillet. Add chicken; cook for 8 to 10 minutes or until chicken is tender and no longer pink, turning to brown evenly. Remove chicken; cover to keep warm.

2

Add orange-grapefruit juice or orange juice, vermouth or white wine, and marmalade to the skillet. Bring to boiling; reduce heat. Boil gently about 3 minutes or until liquid is reduced by half. Return chicken and leek to skillet, turning chicken to coat with glaze. Heat through.

3

To serve, if desired, arrange chicken over hot cooked couscous or rice. Spoon leek mixture over chicken.

Nutrition Facts per serving: 164 calories, 5 g total fat, 45 mg cholesterol, 43 mg sodium, 12 g carbohydrate, 16 g protein.

FRIED CHICKEN WITH GRAVY

Keeping the amount of cooking oil in check and using evaporated fat-free milk means this home-style favorite has only 8 grams of fat per serving.

Start to Finish: 30 minutes **Makes:** 6 servings

- **1/4 cup all-purpose flour**
- **1 1/2 teaspoons snipped fresh thyme or 1/2 teaspoon dried thyme, crushed**
- **1/2 teaspoon salt**
- **1/2 teaspoon paprika**
- **1/8 to 1/4 teaspoon ground black pepper**
- **6 medium skinless, boneless chicken breast halves (about 1 1/2 pounds total)**
- **2 tablespoons cooking oil**
- **1/2 cup evaporated fat-free milk**
- **1/2 cup reduced-sodium chicken broth**
- **Paprika (optional)**
- **Fresh thyme sprigs (optional)**

1

In a heavy plastic bag combine flour, the snipped or dried thyme, salt, the 1/2 teaspoon paprika, and the pepper. Add chicken pieces, 2 at a time; shake to coat. Remove chicken from bag, shaking off excess coating into the bag. Reserve the remaining flour mixture.

2

In a 12-inch skillet heat oil. Cook chicken in hot oil over medium heat for 8 to 10 minutes or until chicken is tender and no longer pink, turning to brown evenly. Drain chicken on paper towels. Cover to keep warm. Discard drippings in skillet.

3

For gravy, in a small bowl slowly stir evaporated milk into reserved flour mixture. Stir in broth; add mixture to skillet. Cook and stir until thickened and bubbly. Cook and stir 1 minute more.

4

To serve, spoon gravy over chicken. If desired, sprinkle with additional paprika and garnish with fresh thyme sprigs.

Nutrition Facts per serving: 198 calories, 8 g total fat, 60 mg cholesterol, 310 mg sodium, 6 g carbohydrate, 24 g protein.

GINGER AND PEACH CHICKEN

Peaches, water chestnuts, and pea pods team up with awesome results in this low-fat entrée.

Start to Finish: 20 minutes **Makes:** 4 servings

- **Nonstick cooking spray**
- **4 small skinless, boneless chicken breast halves (about 12 ounces total)**
- **1 6-ounce package frozen pea pods**
- **1 15-ounce can peach slices in light syrup**
- **1 tablespoon reduced-sodium soy sauce**
- **2 teaspoons cornstarch**
- **1 teaspoon grated fresh ginger or 1/4 teaspoon ground ginger**
- **Dash ground red pepper**
- **1/2 of an 8-ounce can (1/2 cup) sliced water chestnuts, drained**
- **2 cups hot cooked rice**

1

Coat an unheated large nonstick skillet with nonstick cooking spray. Heat over medium heat. Cook chicken in hot skillet for 8 to 10 minutes or until chicken is tender and no longer pink, turning to brown evenly. Remove from skillet; cover to keep warm.

2

Meanwhile, cook pea pods according to package directions. Drain peaches, reserving syrup. Add enough water to syrup to equal 1 cup liquid. Stir in soy sauce, cornstarch, ginger, and red pepper. Add to skillet. Cook and stir until thickened and bubbly. Cook and stir for 1 minute more. Gently stir in peaches and water chestnuts; heat through.

3

To serve, drain pea pods. Arrange rice, chicken, and pea pods on 4 dinner plates. Spoon peach mixture over chicken.

Nutrition Facts per serving: 288 calories, 3 g total fat, 45 mg cholesterol, 182 mg sodium, 45 g carbohydrate, 21 g protein.

MOSASSES-ORANGE GLAZE CHICKEN

Orange juice concentrate and molasses dress up chicken with a rich golen finish and a subtle citrus flavor

Prep: 5 minutes **Broil:** 12 minutes **Makes:** 4 servings

2 tablespoons frozen orange juice concentrate, thawed
2 tablespoons molasses
¼ teaspoon onion powder
4 medium skinless, boneless chicken breast halves (about 1 pound total) or 8 small skinless, boneless chicken thighs
Salt
Ground black pepper
Hot cooked spinach fettuccine or plain fettuccine (optional)
Orange peel strips* (optional)

1

For glaze, in a small bowl stir together orange juice concentrate, molasses, and onion powder.

2

Season chicken with salt and pepper. Place chicken on the unheated rack of a broiler pan. Broil 4 to 5 inches from the heat for 6 minutes. Brush with some of the glaze. Turn chicken; brush with remaining glaze. Broil for 6 to 9 minutes more or until chicken is tender and no longer pink. If desired, serve with fettuccine and garnish with orange peel strips.

***Note:** For orange peel strips, use a vegetable peeler to cut thin strips of peel from the surface of an orange. Make sure to remove only the orange part of the peel.

Nutrition Facts per serving: 160 calories, 3 g total fat, 59 mg cholesterol, 56 mg sodium, 10 g carbohydrate, 22 g protein.

TARRAGON CHICKEN AND APPLES

The assertive flavor of tarragon is just the ticket for accenting this chicken-and-apple combination.

Prep: 15 minutes **Cook:** 15 minutes **Makes:** 4 servings

- **1/2 cup apple juice**
- **3/4 teaspoon snipped fresh tarragon or 1/4 teaspoon dried tarragon, crushed**
- **1/2 teaspoon instant chicken bouillon granules**
- **1 clove garlic, minced**
- **Dash ground black pepper**
- **4 small skinless, boneless chicken breast halves (12 ounces total)**
- **1 medium apple, cored and sliced**
- **1/4 cup sliced green onions**
- **1 tablespoon cold water**
- **1 1/2 teaspoons cornstarch**

1

In a large skillet combine the apple juice, tarragon, bouillon granules, garlic, and pepper. Bring to boiling. Add chicken breasts; reduce heat. Cover and simmer for 7 minutes.

2

Turn chicken over; add apple slices and green onions. Cover and simmer for 4 to 5 minutes more or until chicken is tender and no longer pink.

3

With a slotted spoon, remove chicken and apple to a serving platter; keep warm. Reserve cooking liquid in skillet.

4

In a small bowl stir together the cold water and cornstarch. Stir into cooking liquid in skillet. Cook and stir for 2 minutes more. Spoon over chicken and apples.

Nutrition Facts per serving: 128 calories, 3 g total fat, 45 mg cholesterol, 150 mg sodium, 9 g carbohydrate, 16 g protein.

CHICKEN MARSALA

This classic dish has the look and taste of fine cuisine, yet takes only minutes to prepare.

Start to Finish: 20 minutes **Makes:** 4 servings

4 small boneless, skinless chicken breast halves (12 ounces total)
Nonstick cooking spray
1$^1/_2$ cups sliced fresh mushrooms
2 tablespoons sliced green onion
2 tablespoons water
$^1/_4$ teaspoon salt
$^1/_4$ cup dry Marsala or dry sherry

1

Place each chicken breast half, boned side up, between 2 pieces of plastic wrap. Using the flat side of a meat mallet, lightly pound chicken to about $^1/_4$-inch thickness, working from center to edges. Remove plastic wrap.

2

Coat a large skillet with nonstick cooking spray. Preheat skillet over medium heat. Add 2 chicken breast halves. Cook over medium heat for 4 to 6 minutes or until tender and no longer pink, turning to brown evenly. Transfer to a platter; keep warm. Repeat with remaining chicken.

3

Carefully add mushrooms, green onion, the water, and salt to skillet. Cook and stir over medium heat about 3 minutes or until mushrooms are tender and most of the liquid has evaporated. Add Marsala or sherry to skillet. Heat through. Spoon vegetables and sauce over chicken.

Nutrition Facts per serving: 161 calories, 3 g total fat, 45 mg cholesterol, 175 mg sodium, 2 g carbohydrate, 17 g protein.

HONEY-GINGER CRUSTED CHICKEN

This oven-fried chicken is crisp and flavorful like skillet-fried, but with fewer calories and less fat.

Prep: 10 minutes **Bake:** 18 minutes **Makes:** 4 servings

Nonstick cooking spray
4 small skinless, boneless chicken breast halves (about 12 ounces total)
1 tablespoon honey
1 tablespoon orange juice
1/4 teaspoon ground ginger
1/4 teaspoon ground black pepper
Dash ground red pepper (optional)
3/4 cup cornflakes, crushed
1/2 teaspoon dried parsley flakes

1

Coat a shallow baking pan with nonstick cooking spray. Place chicken breasts in baking pan. In a small bowl combine honey, orange juice, ginger, black pepper, and, if desired, red pepper. Brush honey mixture over chicken. Combine cornflakes and parsley flakes. Sprinkle cornflake mixture over chicken.

2

Bake, uncovered, in a 350°F oven for 18 to 20 minutes or until chicken is tender and no longer pink.

Nutrition Facts per serving: 127 calories, 3 g total fat, 45 mg cholesterol, 94 mg sodium, 8 g carbohydrate, 17 g protein.

LEMON CHICKEN

Here's a reduced-fat version of the Asian restaurant classic.

Start to Finish: 25 minutes **Makes:** 4 servings

- **4 medium skinless, boneless chicken breast halves (about 1 pound total)**
- **1/3 cup all-purpose flour**
- **1/4 teaspoon ground black pepper**
- **2 tablespoons margarine or butter**
- **1 cup chicken broth**
- **1/4 cup lemon juice**
- **1 tablespoon cornstarch**
- **2 green onions, sliced**
- **Lemon slices, cut in half (optional)**
- **Hot cooked couscous (optional)**
- **Cooked artichoke halves (optional)**

1

Place each chicken breast half, boned side up, between 2 sheets of plastic wrap. Using the flat side of a meat mallet, lightly pound chicken to 1/4-inch thickness, working from center to edges. Remove plastic wrap. In a shallow dish stir together flour and pepper. Lightly coat each piece of chicken with the flour mixture.

2

In a large skillet cook chicken in hot margarine or butter over medium heat for 4 to 6 minutes or until chicken is tender and no longer pink, turning to brown evenly. Remove chicken from skillet. Cover to keep warm.

3

For sauce, in a small bowl stir together broth, lemon juice, and cornstarch. Add to skillet. Cook and stir over medium heat until thickened and bubbly. Cook and stir for 2 minutes more. Stir in green onions.

4

To serve, if desired, top chicken with lemon slices. Serve chicken with sauce, and, if desired, hot cooked couscous. If desired, garnish with artichoke halves.

Nutrition Facts per serving: 226 calories, 9 g total fat, 60 mg cholesterol, 315 mg sodium, 10 g carbohydrate, 24 g protein.

SAUTÉED CHICKEN WITH BRANDIED FRUIT AND ALMONDS

This elegant fruited chicken gets just a bit of fire from the ground red pepper.

Start to Finish: 30 minutes **Makes:** 4 servings

- **4 medium skinless, boneless chicken breast halves (about 1 pound total)**
- **1/4 cup all-purpose flour**
- **1/4 teaspoon salt**
- **1/8 teaspoon ground red pepper**
- **1 tablespoon olive oil**
- **1 tablespoon butter or margarine**
- **3 medium nectarines, plums, peaches,* or pears, pitted or cored and cut into thin wedges**
- **3 tablespoons brandy**
- **1 tablespoon lemon juice**
- **2 tablespoons water**
- **2 tablespoons sliced almonds, toasted**
- **Fresh oregano sprigs (optional)**

1

Place each chicken piece, boned side up, between 2 pieces of plastic wrap. Using the flat side of a meat mallet, lightly pound chicken to 1/4-inch thickness, working from center to edges. Remove plastic wrap. In a shallow bowl combine flour, salt, and red pepper. Coat chicken pieces with flour mixture.

2

In a large skillet heat oil and butter or margarine over medium heat. Cook chicken in hot oil mixture for 6 to 8 minutes or until chicken is tender and no longer pink, turning to brown evenly. Remove skillet from heat. Transfer chicken to a serving platter; cover to keep warm. Add fruit, brandy, lemon juice, and the water to skillet. Return to heat and cook for 1 minute, stirring gently.

3

To serve, slice chicken and arrange slices in 4 bowls or on 4 dinner plates. Serve the fruit mixture over chicken. Sprinkle with almonds. If desired, garnish with oregano sprigs.

Nutrition Facts per serving: 303 calories, 12 g total fat, 67 mg cholesterol, 217 mg sodium, 19 g carbohydrate, 24 g protein.

***Note:** If desired, peel peaches.

CILANTRO CHICKEN WITH PEANUTS

Try dried chipotle, pasilla, or ancho peppers in this fabulous chicken dish that's a little bit Tex-Mex and a little bit Asian.

Start to Finish: 25 minutes **Makes:** 4 servings

2 teaspoons roasted peanut oil
1 pound skinless, boneless chicken breasts, cut into 1-inch strips
1 ounce honey-roasted peanuts
1 to 2 dried red chile peppers, crumbled
1 tablespoon soy sauce
2 teaspoons rice vinegar
1 teaspoon toasted sesame oil
1½ cups packed fresh cilantro leaves
4 cups finely shredded Napa cabbage or 2 cups hot cooked rice
Fresh cilantro sprigs (optional)
Lime slices, halved (optional)

1

In a heavy 10-inch skillet heat peanut oil over high heat. Cook and stir chicken in hot oil for 2 minutes. Add honey-roasted peanuts and crumbled peppers. Cook and stir for 3 minutes more or until chicken is no longer pink.

2

Add soy sauce, vinegar, and sesame oil. Cook and stir for 2 minutes more. Remove from heat. Stir in cilantro leaves.

3

To serve, spoon chicken mixture over cabbage or rice. If desired, garnish with cilantro sprigs and lime slices.

Nutrition Facts per serving: 254 calories, 8 g total fat, 49 mg cholesterol, 322 mg sodium, 20 g carbohydrate, 25 g protein.

CHICKEN WITH ROQUEFORT SAUCE

French Roquefort cheese lends a touch of old-world elegance to this creamy chicken dish.

Prep: 12 minutes **Grill:** 12 minutes **Makes:** 4 servings

- **1/2 cup plain fat-free yogurt**
- **1/4 cup chopped red onion**
- **2 tablespoons crumbled Roquefort or other blue cheese**
- **1 tablespoon snipped fresh chives**
- **1/8 teaspoon ground white pepper**
- **2 small pears, halved lengthwise, cored, and stemmed**
- **Lemon juice**
- **4 medium skinless, boneless chicken breast halves (about 1 pound total)**
- **Salt**
- **Ground black pepper**

1

For sauce, in a small bowl combine yogurt, onion, Roquefort cheese, chives, and white pepper. Cover and refrigerate until ready to serve. Brush the cut sides of pears with lemon juice. Set aside.

2

Sprinkle chicken with salt and black pepper. Grill chicken on the lightly greased rack of an uncovered grill directly over medium heat for 5 minutes. Turn chicken. Add pears to grill, cut sides down. Grill chicken and pears for 7 to 10 minutes or until chicken is tender and no longer pink. Serve chicken and pears with sauce.

Nutrition Facts per serving: 199 calories, 5 g total fat, 63 mg cholesterol, 168 mg sodium, 14 g carbohydrate, 25 g protein.

MEDITERRANEAN CHICKEN AND PASTA

Artichokes, garlic, olives, and feta cheese give this pasta dish the flavors of the Greek isles. *(Pictured on page 85.)*

Start to Finish: 25 minutes **Makes:** 4 servings

- **1 6-ounce jar marinated artichoke hearts**
- **1 tablespoon olive oil**
- **12 ounces skinless, boneless chicken breasts, cut into 3/4-inch cubes**
- **3 cloves garlic, thinly sliced**
- **1/4 cup chicken broth**
- **1/4 cup dry white wine**
- **1 tablespoon small fresh oregano leaves or 1 teaspoon dried oregano, crushed**
- **1 7-ounce jar roasted red sweet peppers, drained and cut into strips**
- **1/4 cup pitted kalamata olives**
- **3 cups hot cooked campanelle or penne (mostaccioli)**
- **1/4 cup crumbled feta cheese (optional)**

1

Drain artichokes, reserving marinade. Set aside. In a large skillet heat oil over medium-high heat. Cook and stir chicken and garlic in hot oil until chicken is browned. Add the reserved artichoke marinade, broth, wine, and, if using, dried oregano.

2

Bring to boiling; reduce heat. Cover and simmer for 10 minutes. Stir in artichokes, roasted peppers, olives, and, if using, fresh oregano. Heat through.

3

To serve, spoon the chicken mixture over pasta. If desired, sprinkle with feta cheese.

Nutrition Facts per serving: 337 calories, 9 g total fat, 49 mg cholesterol, 323 mg sodium, 36 g carbohydrate, 26 g protein.

CHICKEN AND PENNE WITH BASIL SAUCE

If you can't get fresh basil, substitute fresh thyme, sage, or tarragon.

Start to Finish: 25 minutes **Makes:** 4 servings

1¼ cups reduced-sodium chicken broth
4 teaspoons cornstarch
⅛ teaspoon ground black pepper
2 cups dried penne (mostaccioli) or corkscrew macaroni (rotini)
Nonstick cooking spray
1 medium red sweet pepper, cut into thin, bite-size strips
1 medium yellow or green sweet pepper, cut into thin, bite-size strips
3 cloves garlic, minced
1 tablespoon cooking oil
12 ounces skinless, boneless chicken breasts, cut into 1-inch cubes
¼ cup lightly packed fresh basil leaves, cut into thin shreds
2 tablespoons shredded Parmesan cheese
Fresh basil sprigs (optional)

1

In a small bowl combine broth, cornstarch, and black pepper. Set aside.

2

Cook pasta according to package directions, omitting any oil and salt. Drain pasta. Return to pan. Cover; keep warm.

3

Coat an unheated large skillet with nonstick cooking spray. Heat over medium heat. Stir-fry sweet peppers and garlic in hot skillet for 2 to 3 minutes or until sweet peppers are crisp-tender. Remove from skillet. Add the oil to skillet; increase heat to medium-high. Stir-fry the chicken in hot oil for 3 to 4 minutes or until chicken is no longer pink.

4

Stir broth mixture; add to skillet. Cook and stir until thickened and bubbly. Return sweet peppers to skillet; add shredded basil. Cook and stir for 2 minutes more.

5

To serve, toss chicken mixture with hot cooked pasta. Sprinkle with Parmesan cheese. If desired, garnish with basil sprigs.

Nutrition Facts per serving: 330 calories, 8 g total fat, 47 mg cholesterol, 282 mg sodium, 39 g carbohydrate, 24 g protein.

GRILLED CHICKEN AND VEGETABLE KABOBS

Grilling the chicken and vegetables on separate skewers means you can take the vegetables off when they're done and let the chicken cook longer if needed.

Start to Finish: 30 minutes **Makes:** 4 servings

- **1 pound skinless, boneless chicken breasts**
- **4 medium fresh mushrooms**
- **3 green onions, cut into 1-inch pieces**
- **1/2 of a medium red or green sweet pepper, cut into 1 1/2-inch pieces**
- **1/2 of a medium orange or yellow sweet pepper, cut into 1 1/2-inch pieces**
- **1/2 cup salsa catsup or regular catsup**
- **2 tablespoons jalapeño jelly**
- **Thinly sliced green onion (optional)**
- **Hot cooked rice (optional)**

1

Cut chicken lengthwise into 1/2-inch strips. On 2 long or 4 short skewers, loosely thread chicken accordion-style. On 1 long or 2 short skewers, alternately thread the mushrooms and green onion pieces, leaving 1/4 inch space between pieces. On 1 long or 2 short skewers, thread the sweet pepper pieces, leaving 1/4 inch space between pieces.

2

For sauce, in a small saucepan heat the catsup and jelly. Brush over chicken and vegetables.

3

Grill skewers on the rack of an uncovered grill directly over medium coals for 10 to 12 minutes or until the chicken is tender and no longer pink and the vegetables are crisp-tender, turning once and brushing once with sauce halfway through grilling. (Or place skewers on unheated rack of a broiler pan. Broil 4 to 5 inches from heat for 12 to 14 minutes, turning once and brushing once with sauce halfway through broiling.) Discard any remaining sauce.

4

To serve, if desired, stir sliced green onion into hot rice. Serve kabobs over rice mixture.

Nutrition Facts per serving: 183 calories, 4 g total fat, 59 mg cholesterol, 314 mg sodium, 15 g carbohydrate, 23 g protein.

MOROCCAN CHICKEN AND VEGETABLE STEW

Pattypan squash and carrots cook in no time. For even cooking, cut larger vegetables in half.

Start to Finish: 25 minutes **Makes:** 4 servings

- **1 cup quick-cooking couscous or flavored couscous**
- **1 tablespoon olive oil**
- **12 ounces boneless, skinless chicken thighs or breasts, cut into 1-inch pieces**
- **1/3 cup sliced cipollini onions or shallots**
- **3 cloves garlic, minced**
- **1/2 teaspoon salt**
- **1/2 teaspoon paprika**
- **1/2 teaspoon ground cumin**
- **1/4 teaspoon ground cinnamon**
- **1/4 teaspoon ground saffron or ground turmeric**
- **1/8 teaspoon ground red pepper**
- **6 ounces baby pattypan or asparagus squash or 1 1/2 cups sliced zucchini**
- **1 cup thin packaged, peeled baby carrots**
- **1 cup reduced-sodium chicken broth**
- **1/4 cup golden or dark raisins**

1

Cook couscous according to package directions, omitting any oil or salt. Keep warm.

2

Meanwhile, in a large nonstick skillet heat oil over medium-high heat. Cook and stir chicken, onions, and garlic in hot oil for 2 minutes. In a small bowl combine salt, paprika, cumin, cinnamon, saffron or turmeric, and red pepper; sprinkle evenly over mixture in skillet. Cook and stir about 2 minutes more or until chicken is no longer pink.

3

Cut any large pieces of squash and carrots in half. Add squash, carrots, broth, and raisins to skillet. Bring to boiling; reduce heat. Cover and simmer for 6 to 8 minutes or until vegetables are crisp-tender.

4

To serve, ladle chicken mixture over couscous in bowls.

Nutrition Facts per serving: 363 calories, 7 g total fat, 45 mg cholesterol, 496 mg sodium, 51 g carbohydrate, 24 g protein.

CURRIED CHICKEN SOUP

No leftover cooked chicken? Buy a roasted bird at your supermarket's deli counter or look for frozen cooked chicken in the freezer case.

Start to Finish: 20 minutes **Makes:** 5 servings

5 cups water
1 3-ounce package chicken-flavored ramen noodles
2 to 3 teaspoons curry powder
1 cup sliced fresh mushrooms
2 cups cubed cooked chicken
1 medium apple, cored and coarsely chopped
1/2 of an 8-ounce can (1/2 cup) sliced water chestnuts, drained

1

In a large saucepan combine the water, the flavoring packet from the ramen noodles, and the curry powder. Bring to boiling.

2

Break up noodles and add to mixture in saucepan along with the mushrooms. Return to boiling; reduce heat. Simmer, uncovered, for 3 minutes.

3

Stir in chicken, apple, and water chestnuts. Heat through.

Nutrition Facts per serving: 217 calories, 8 g total fat, 54 mg cholesterol, 449 mg sodium, 17 g carbohydrate, 20 g protein.

CURRIED CHICKEN AND FRUIT SALAD

Another time, try this quick-fixing salad with raspberries, blueberries, or coarsely chopped nectarines in place of the strawberries.

Start to Finish: 20 minutes **Makes:** 4 servings

2 cups fresh strawberry halves
1 11-ounce can pineapple tidbits and mandarin orange sections, drained, or one 11-ounce can mandarin orange sections, drained
1/4 cup fat-free mayonnaise dressing or salad dressing
1/4 cup fat-free dairy sour cream
2 tablespoons frozen orange juice concentrate
3/4 to 1 teaspoon curry powder
4 to 5 tablespoons fat-free milk
6 cups torn mixed salad greens
8 ounces cooked chicken, cubed, or cooked roast beef, thinly sliced and rolled up
Toasted coconut (optional)

1

In a medium bowl toss together strawberries and drained canned fruit. Set aside.

2

For dressing, in a small bowl stir together the mayonnaise dressing or salad dressing, sour cream, orange juice concentrate, and curry powder. Stir in enough milk to make of drizzling consistency.

3

Line 4 dinner plates with torn mixed greens. Top with fruit mixture and cooked chicken or beef. Drizzle with the dressing. If desired, garnish with toasted coconut.

Nutrition Facts per serving: 233 calories, 5 g total fat, 51 mg cholesterol, 288 mg sodium, 28 g carbohydrate, 20 g protein.

CHICKEN AND VEGETABLE SALAD

Remember this salad when it's too hot to cook. Just add breadsticks, iced tea, and a fresh fruit dessert, and the meal is complete.

Start to Finish: 25 minutes **Makes:** 4 servings

- **1/2 cup low-fat cottage cheese or fat-free cottage cheese**
- **1 tablespoon catsup**
- **1 hard-cooked egg, chopped (optional)**
- **1 tablespoon thinly sliced green onion**
- **1 tablespoon sweet pickle relish**
- **1/8 teaspoon salt**
- **1 1/2 cups chopped cooked chicken (about 8 ounces)**
- **1/2 cup sliced celery**
- **1/2 cup chopped red or green sweet pepper**
- **Lettuce leaves**
- **2 tablespoons sliced almonds, toasted**

1

For dressing, in a food processor bowl combine cottage cheese and catsup. Cover and process until smooth; transfer to a small bowl. Stir in egg (if desired), green onion, pickle relish, and salt. Set aside.

2

In a medium bowl combine chicken, celery, and sweet pepper. Add dressing and gently toss to mix.

3

To serve, divide salad among 4 lettuce-lined dinner plates. Sprinkle with the almonds.

Nutrition Facts per serving: 170 calories, 6 g total fat, 53 mg cholesterol, 326 mg sodium, 6 g carbohydrate, 22 g protein.

FABULOUS FOCACCIA SANDWICHES

With deli-roasted chicken, you can put these sophisticated sandwiches together in a flash.

Start to Finish: 15 minutes **Makes:** 4 servings

- **1 8- to 10-inch tomato or onion Italian flatbread (focaccia) or 1 loaf sourdough bread**
- **3 to 4 tablespoons light mayonnaise dressing or salad dressing**
- **1 to 2 tablespoons shredded fresh basil**
- **1½ cups packaged prewashed fresh spinach**
- **1½ cups sliced or shredded deli-cooked rotisserie chicken**
- **½ of a 7-ounce jar (about ½ cup) roasted red sweet peppers, drained and cut into wide strips**

1

Using a long serrated knife, cut bread in half horizontally. In a small bowl stir together mayonnaise dressing or salad dressing and basil. Spread cut sides of bread halves with dressing mixture.

2

Layer spinach, chicken, and roasted sweet peppers between bread halves. Cut into quarters.

Nutrition Facts per serving: 370 calories, 11 g total fat, 51 mg cholesterol, 148 mg sodium, 43 g carbohydrate, 25 g protein.

CHICKEN FAJITAS

Chicken breasts and low-fat yogurt keep these easy fajitas light.

Start to Finish: 25 minutes **Makes:** 4 servings

- **8 7- to 8-inch flour tortillas**
- **Nonstick cooking spray**
- **1 small onion, sliced and separated into rings**
- **2 cloves garlic, minced**
- **1 medium red or green sweet pepper, cut into thin, bite-size strips**
- **1 tablespoon cooking oil**
- **3 small skinless, boneless chicken breasts, cut into bite-size strips (about 9 ounces total)**
- **1/3 cup bottled salsa**
- **2 cups shredded lettuce**
- **1/4 cup plain low-fat yogurt or light dairy sour cream**
- **1 green onion, thinly sliced**

1

Wrap tortillas in foil. Heat in a 350°F oven for 10 minutes to soften.

2

Meanwhile, coat an unheated large skillet with nonstick cooking spray. Heat over medium-high heat. Stir-fry onion rings and garlic in hot skillet for 2 minutes. Add the sweet pepper; stir-fry for 1 to 2 minutes more or until vegetables are crisp-tender. Remove from skillet. Add oil to skillet. Stir-fry chicken in hot oil for 3 to 5 minutes or until chicken is tender and no longer pink. Return vegetables to skillet. Add salsa. Cook and stir until heated through.

3

To serve, divide chicken mixture evenly among tortillas. Top with lettuce. Spoon yogurt or sour cream on top and sprinkle with green onion. Roll up tortillas.

Nutrition Facts per serving: 307 calories, 11 g total fat, 34 mg cholesterol, 357 mg sodium, 35 g carbohydrate, 18 g protein.

TURKEY PICCATA

Serving spinach linguine or noodles with this lemony turkey makes for a more substantial entrée and adds only 105 calories per ¾-cup serving.

Start to Finish: 25 minutes **Makes:** 4 servings

- **4 2½- to 3-ounce turkey breast cutlets or slices**
- **¼ teaspoon salt**
- **¼ teaspoon coarsely ground black pepper**
- **Nonstick cooking spray**
- **1 teaspoon olive oil**
- **2 to 3 cloves garlic, minced**
- **¾ cup reduced-sodium chicken broth**
- **1 tablespoon all-purpose flour**
- **2 tablespoons snipped fresh parsley**
- **4 teaspoons lemon juice**
- **Hot cooked spinach linguine or noodles (optional)**
- **Lemon wedges (optional)**

1

Place each turkey piece between 2 pieces of plastic wrap. Using the flat side of a meat mallet, lightly pound turkey to an ⅛-inch thickness, working from center to edges. Remove plastic wrap. Sprinkle turkey with salt and pepper.

2

Coat an unheated large nonstick skillet with nonstick cooking spray. Heat over medium-high heat. Cook 2 of the turkey pieces in hot skillet for 2 to 3 minutes or until lightly browned and centers are no longer pink, turning once halfway through cooking. Transfer to a serving platter; cover to keep warm. Add the oil to skillet. Repeat with remaining turkey pieces. Remove to platter, reserving drippings in skillet.

3

For sauce, add garlic to skillet; cook 30 seconds. In a screw-top jar combine broth and flour. Cover and shake well. Add to skillet; cook and stir until thickened and bubbly. Cook and stir for 1 minute more. Stir in parsley and lemon juice; heat through.

4

To serve, spoon sauce over turkey. If desired, serve with hot cooked linguine or noodles and garnish with lemon wedges.

Nutrition Facts per serving: 110 calories, 3 g total fat, 37 mg cholesterol, 289 mg sodium, 3 g carbohydrate, 17 g protein.

FRESH TOMATO AND TURKEY PIZZA

No need to hold back with this great pizza. One-fourth of the pizza has fewer than 300 calories.

Prep: 15 minutes **Bake:** 13 minutes **Makes:** 4 servings

- Nonstick cooking spray
- 1 tablespoon cornmeal
- 1 10-ounce package refrigerated pizza dough
- 3 medium plum tomatoes, thinly sliced
- 4 ounces cooked turkey breast or smoked turkey breast, cut into thin strips
- 3 tablespoons snipped fresh basil
- 1/4 teaspoon coarsely ground black pepper
- 1 cup shredded reduced-fat mozzarella cheese (4 ounces)

1

Coat a 12-inch pizza pan with nonstick cooking spray. Sprinkle cornmeal over bottom of pan. Press refrigerated dough into pan, building up edges. Arrange tomato slices and turkey strips on the dough. Sprinkle with basil and pepper. Sprinkle cheese on top.

2

Bake in a 425°F oven for 13 to 18 minutes or until cheese is bubbly.

Nutrition Facts per serving: 288 calories, 8 g total fat, 39 mg cholesterol, 449 mg sodium, 32 g carbohydrate, 21 g protein.

TURKEY WITH MIXED DRIED FRUIT

The mixed dried fruit adds a hint of sweetness to these moist, tender turkey steaks.

Start to Finish: 25 minutes **Makes:** 4 servings

Nonstick cooking spray
12 ounces turkey breast tenderloin steaks*
1 cup apple juice or apple cider
1 cup mixed dried fruit bits
1/2 cup chopped onion
1 1/2 teaspoons snipped fresh thyme or 1/2 teaspoon dried thyme, crushed
2 cloves garlic, minced
1/2 cup apple juice or apple cider
1 tablespoon cornstarch
Hot cooked orzo or rice (optional)
Fresh thyme sprigs (optional)

1

Coat an unheated large skillet with nonstick cooking spray. Preheat over medium-high heat. Add turkey; cook for 8 to 10 minutes or until tender and no longer pink, turning once halfway through cooking. Remove from skillet.

2

For sauce, in the same skillet combine the 1 cup apple juice or cider, the dried fruit bits, onion, the snipped thyme, and garlic. Bring to boiling; reduce heat. Cover and simmer for 2 to 4 minutes or just until fruit bits are tender.

3

In a small bowl stir together the 1/2 cup apple juice or cider and the cornstarch. Add to mixture in skillet. Cook and stir until thickened and bubbly. Cook and stir for 2 minutes more. Return turkey to skillet; heat through. If desired, serve turkey and sauce with orzo or rice and garnish with thyme sprigs.

***Note:** If you can't find turkey breast tenderloin steaks, buy 2 turkey breast tenderloins and split them in half lengthwise.

Nutrition Facts per serving: 234 calories, 2 g total fat, 37 mg cholesterol, 60 mg sodium, 39 g carbohydrate, 18 g protein.

TURKEY AND CHILE PEPPER STIR-FRY

Use Anaheim peppers to give this dish a mild pepper kick or jalapeños to give it a jolt.

Start to Finish: 25 minutes **Makes:** 4 servings

- **1/3 cup water**
- **2 tablespoons reduced-sodium soy sauce**
- **2 teaspoons cornstarch**
- **Nonstick cooking spray**
- **4 cups chopped bok choy**
- **1 medium red or green sweet pepper, cut into thin, bite-size strips**
- **1/4 cup finely chopped seeded Anaheim pepper or 1 tablespoon finely chopped seeded jalapeño pepper***
- **1 1/2 cups cooked turkey breast, cut into bite-size strips (about 8 ounces)**
- **1/4 cup sliced water chestnuts**
- **2 cups hot cooked rice**

1

For sauce, in a small bowl combine the water, soy sauce, and cornstarch. Set aside.

2

Coat an unheated wok or large skillet with nonstick cooking spray. Heat over medium-high heat. Stir-fry bok choy, sweet pepper, and Anaheim or jalapeño pepper for 2 to 3 minutes or until peppers are crisp-tender. Remove from wok.

3

Add turkey to wok; stir-fry about 2 minutes or until heated through. Push turkey from center of wok. Stir sauce mixture; add to center of wok. Cook and stir until thickened and bubbly.

4

Return vegetables to wok; add water chestnuts. Stir to coat all ingredients; cook about 1 minute more or until heated through.

5

To serve, spoon turkey mixture over hot cooked rice.

Nutrition Facts per serving: 255 calories, 6 g total fat, 54 mg cholesterol, 312 mg sodium, 30 g carbohydrate, 20 g protein.

***Note:** Because chile peppers, such as Anaheims and jalapeños, contain volatile oils that can burn your skin and eyes, avoid direct contact with them as much as possible. When working with chile peppers, wear plastic or rubber gloves. If your bare hands do touch the chile peppers, wash your hands and nails well with soap and water.

SWEET-SOUR TURKEY SALAD

Spreadable fruit mixed with a little vinegar, soy sauce, and ginger makes for a lively no-fat dressing. Although this recipe uses peach or apricot spreadable fruit, you can try any flavor you like.

Start to Finish: 25 minutes **Makes:** 4 servings

- **1/2 cup peach or apricot spreadable fruit**
- **2 tablespoons cider vinegar**
- **1 tablespoon reduced-sodium soy sauce**
- **1/8 teaspoon ground ginger**
- **6 cups torn mixed greens**
- **6 ounces cooked boneless turkey breast, cut onto thin bite-size strips (about 1 1/4 cups)**
- **1 11-ounce can mandarin orange sections, drained, or 2 medium oranges, sectioned**
- **1 cup broccoli florets**
- **1 cup cauliflower florets**

1

For dressing, in a small saucepan stir together spreadable fruit, vinegar, soy sauce, and ginger. Cook and stir over low heat until bubbly. Remove from heat. Set aside to cool slightly.

2

In a large bowl toss together greens, turkey breast, orange sections, broccoli, and cauliflower. Divide greens mixture among 4 plates. Drizzle with dressing.

Nutrition Facts per serving: 204 calories, 1 g total fat, 35 mg cholesterol, 180 mg sodium, 39 g carbohydrate, 16 g protein.

TURKEY AND NECTARINE SALAD

Buttermilk gives this refreshing salad extra tang. If you don't have buttermilk on hand, regular fat-free milk works just fine.

Start to Finish: 25 minutes **Makes:** 4 servings

- **2/3 cup buttermilk**
- **2 tablespoons light mayonnaise dressing or salad dressing**
- **2 to 3 teaspoons snipped fresh dill or 1/4 to 1/2 teaspoon dried dill**
- **1/8 teaspoon salt**
- **1/8 teaspoon onion powder**
- **1/8 teaspoon garlic powder**
- **6 cups torn mixed salad greens**
- **8 ounces cooked turkey breast, thinly sliced**
- **2 medium nectarines, pitted and sliced, or 2 medium peaches, peeled, pitted, and sliced**
- **1/4 cup chopped red sweet pepper**
- **Snipped fresh dill (optional)**

1

For dressing, in a small bowl gradually stir buttermilk into mayonnaise dressing or salad dressing until smooth. Stir in the 2 to 3 teaspoons snipped dill or 1/4 to 1/2 teaspoon dried dill, salt, onion powder, and garlic powder.

2

To serve, arrange greens on 4 dinner plates. Top with turkey and nectarines or peaches. Drizzle dressing over salads. Sprinkle with sweet pepper. If desired, sprinkle with additional snipped dill.

Nutrition Facts per serving: 180 calories, 5 g total fat, 41 mg cholesterol, 228 mg sodium, 13 g carbohydrate, 21 g protein.

TALL TURKEY SANDWICH

For a really lively turkey sandwich, stir 1 teaspoon prepared horseradish into the yogurt spread.

Start to Finish: 10 minutes **Makes:** 1 serving

- **1 tablespoon fat-free plain yogurt**
- **2 teaspoons horseradish mustard**
- **2 slices multigrain bread, toasted**
- **3 or 4 leaves lettuce**
- **2 to 3 ounces cooked turkey breast, sliced**
- **2 tomato slices**
- **1 yellow sweet pepper slice**
- **1/4 cup fresh pea pods**

1

In a small bowl stir together yogurt and horseradish mustard; spread on 1 of the toasted bread slices.

2

Layer lettuce, turkey, tomato, and sweet pepper on top of bread. Add the pea pods and remaining toasted bread slice.

Nutrition Facts per serving: 244 calories, 2 g total fat, 47 mg cholesterol, 380 mg sodium, 32 g carbohydrate, 26 g protein.

SLIMMED SKILLET-STYLE LASAGNA

Here's lasagna done right—with all the flavor of the traditional favorite but with only 235 calories and 8 grams of fat per serving.

Start to Finish: 35 minutes **Makes:** 6 serving

- **8 ounces uncooked ground turkey sausage**
- **1/2 cup chopped onion**
- **2 cups bottled spaghetti sauce**
- **1 cup water**
- **2 cups dried wide noodles**
- **1 1/2 cups coarsely chopped zucchini**
- **1/2 cup fat-free ricotta cheese**
- **2 tablespoons grated Parmesan or Romano cheese**
- **1 tablespoon snipped fresh parsley**
- **1/2 cup shredded reduced-fat mozzarella cheese (2 ounces)**

1

In a large skillet cook sausage and onion until sausage is browned, breaking up sausage during cooking. Drain off fat. Stir in spaghetti sauce and the water. Bring to boiling. Stir in uncooked noodles and zucchini. Return to boiling; reduce heat. Cover and simmer about 12 minutes or until noodles are tender, stirring occasionally.

2

Meanwhile, in a small bowl stir together ricotta cheese, Parmesan or Romano cheese, and parsley.

3

Drop cheese mixture into 6 mounds over the sausage-noodle mixture in the skillet. Sprinkle mounds with mozzarella cheese. Cover and cook on low heat for 4 to 5 minutes or until cheese mixture is heated through. Let stand 10 minutes before serving.

Nutrition Facts per serving: 235 calories, 8 g total fat, 38 mg cholesterol, 418 mg sodium, 26 g carbohydrate, 18 g protein.

FISH & SEAFOOD

Your favorite fish or seafood used in these calorie-trimmed recipes adds up to delectable dining.

Salmon with Fresh Pineapple Salsa
(see recipe, page 174)

SWEET-AND-SOUR FISH

Using poached rather than fried fish helps trim the fat and calories in this Asian favorite.

Start to Finish: 30 minutes **Makes:** 4 servings

- **1 pound fresh or frozen fish steaks (such as halibut, swordfish, or tuna)**
- **2 tablespoons brown sugar**
- **2 tablespoons vinegar**
- **2 tablespoons reduced-sodium soy sauce**
- **4 teaspoons cornstarch**
- **2/3 cup reduced-sodium chicken broth**
- **1 medium green or red sweet pepper, cut into 1-inch squares**
- **1 medium carrot, thinly bias-sliced**
- **1/2 cup red seedless grapes, halved**
- **2 cups hot cooked rice**

1

Thaw fish, if frozen. Rinse fish; pat dry with paper towels. Cut fish into 1-inch pieces. In a large covered saucepan cook fish pieces in boiling water about 5 minutes or just until fish flakes easily with a fork. Drain. Cover to keep warm.

2

In a small bowl combine brown sugar, vinegar, soy sauce, and cornstarch. Set aside. In a medium saucepan combine broth, sweet pepper, and carrot. Bring to boiling; reduce heat. Cover and simmer about 3 minutes or until vegetables are crisp-tender.

3

Stir brown sugar mixture into vegetable mixture. Cook and stir until thickened and bubbly. Cook and stir for 2 minutes more. Gently stir in fish and grapes. Cook about 1 minute more or until heated through.

4

To serve, spoon fish mixture over hot cooked rice.

Nutrition Facts per serving: 294 calories, 3 g total fat, 36 mg cholesterol, 446 mg sodium, 38 g carbohydrate, 27 g protein.

SNAPPER VERACRUZ

To combat the heat of the jalapeños or serranos, serve this colorful dish with boiled new potatoes.

Start to Finish: 30 minutes **Makes:** 6 servings

- **$1\frac{1}{2}$ pounds fresh or frozen skinless red snapper or other fish fillets**
- **1/8 teaspoon salt**
- **1/8 teaspoon ground black pepper**
- **1 tablespoon cooking oil**
- **1 large onion, sliced and separated into rings**
- **1 teaspoon bottled minced garlic or 2 cloves garlic, minced**
- **2 large tomatoes, chopped (2 cups)**
- **1/4 cup sliced pimiento-stuffed green olives**
- **1/4 cup dry white wine**
- **2 tablespoons capers, drained**
- **1 to 2 fresh jalapeño or serrano peppers,* seeded and chopped, or 1 to 2 canned jalapeño peppers, rinsed, drained, seeded, and chopped**
- **1/2 teaspoon sugar**
- **1 bay leaf**
- **Snipped fresh parsley**

1

Thaw fish, if frozen. Rinse fish; pat dry with paper towels. Cut fish into 6 serving-size pieces. Measure thickness of fish. Sprinkle fish fillets with the salt and black pepper.

2

For sauce, in a large skillet heat oil. Cook onion and garlic in hot oil until onion is tender. Stir in tomatoes, olives, wine, capers, jalapeño or serrano peppers, sugar, and bay leaf. Bring to boiling. Add fish to skillet. Return to boiling; reduce heat. Cover and simmer just until fish flakes easily with a fork (allow 4 to 6 minutes per 1/2-inch thickness of fish). Use a slotted spatula to carefully transfer fish from skillet to a serving platter. Cover to keep warm.

3

Boil sauce in skillet for 5 to 6 minutes or until reduced to about 2 cups, stirring occasionally. Discard bay leaf.

4

To serve, spoon some of the sauce onto 6 dinner plates. Top each with a piece of fish. Top fish with more sauce. Sprinkle each serving with parsley.

Nutrition Facts per serving: 174 calories, 5 g total fat, 42 mg cholesterol, 260 mg sodium, 7 g carbohydrate, 24 g protein.

***Note:** Because chile peppers, such as jalapeños and serranos, contain volatile oils that can burn your skin and eyes, avoid direct contact with them as much as possible. When working with chile peppers, wear plastic or rubber gloves. If your bare hands do touch the chile peppers, wash your hands and nails well with soap and water.

TUNA WITH FRESH ORANGE SALSA

The citrus-cilantro salsa accents the earthy flavor of the cumin-rubbed tuna perfectly.

Prep: 20 minutes **Broil:** 8 minutes **Makes:** 4 servings

4 fresh or frozen tuna or sea bass steaks, cut 1 inch thick
1 teaspoon finely shredded orange peel
4 medium oranges, peeled, sectioned, and coarsely chopped
1 large tomato, seeded and chopped
1/4 cup snipped fresh cilantro
2 tablespoons finely chopped green onion
2 tablespoons chopped walnuts, toasted
1 tablespoon lime juice
1/2 teaspoon salt
1/2 teaspoon ground black pepper
1/2 teaspoon ground cumin
1 tablespoon olive oil

1

Thaw fish, if frozen. Rinse fish; pat dry with paper towels. For salsa, in a medium bowl combine the orange peel, oranges, tomato, cilantro, green onion, walnuts, lime juice, 1/4 teaspoon of the salt, and 1/4 teaspoon of the pepper. Set aside.

2

In a small bowl combine cumin, the remaining salt, and the remaining pepper. Brush the fish with oil and sprinkle evenly with the cumin mixture.

3

Lightly grease the unheated rack of a broiler pan. Place fish on rack. Broil 4 inches from the heat for 8 to 12 minutes or just until fish flakes easily with a fork, carefully turning once halfway through broiling.

4

To serve, spoon salsa over fish.

Nutrition Facts per serving: 262 calories, 12 g total fat, 43 mg cholesterol, 343 mg sodium, 11 g carbohydrate, 28 g protein.

ROASTED RED SNAPPER WITH TOMATOES AND FETA CHEESE

Using low-sodium tomatoes helps keep the sodium in check. To cut the salt even more, rinse the feta cheese under cold water.

Prep: 20 minutes **Bake:** 8 minutes **Makes:** 4 servings

- **1 pound fresh or frozen red snapper fillets, about 1 inch thick**
- **1 14½-ounce can low-sodium tomatoes, cut up**
- **8 green onions, sliced**
- **¼ cup thinly sliced celery**
- **2 tablespoons lemon juice**
- **1 teaspoon dried oregano, crushed**
- **Nonstick cooking spray**
- **¼ teaspoon ground black pepper**
- **¼ teaspoon ground coriander**
- **¼ cup crumbled feta cheese (1 ounce)**
- **2 tablespoons sliced ripe olives**
- **Fresh parsley sprigs (optional)**

1

Thaw fish, if frozen. Rinse fish; pat dry with paper towels. Cut into 4 serving-size pieces.

2

For sauce, in a large skillet combine undrained tomatoes, green onions, celery, lemon juice, and oregano. Bring to boiling; reduce heat. Simmer, uncovered, about 15 minutes or until most of the liquid has evaporated.

3

Meanwhile, coat a 2-quart rectangular baking dish with nonstick cooking spray. Place the fish pieces in the dish, tucking under any thin edges for an even thickness. Sprinkle with the pepper and coriander.

4

Bake, uncovered, in a 450°F oven for 8 to 12 minutes or just until fish flakes easily with a fork.

5

To serve, spoon sauce over fish. Sprinkle feta cheese and olives over fish. If desired, garnish with parsley sprigs.

Nutrition Facts per serving: 169 calories, 4 g total fat, 48 mg cholesterol, 189 mg sodium, 7 g carbohydrate, 26 g protein.

CATFISH HOAGIES

Many supermarkets carry fresh farm-raised catfish at the fish counter year-round.

Start to Finish: 25 minutes **Makes:** 4 servings

- **4 3-ounce fresh or frozen catfish fillets**
- **1 tablespoon lime juice**
- **¼ teaspoon ground red pepper**
- **Dash salt**
- **3 tablespoons fat-free or light mayonnaise dressing or salad dressing**
- **1 tablespoon honey mustard**
- **1 12-inch Italian flatbread (focaccia), cut into quarters, split, and toasted***
- **Watercress or lettuce leaves**
- **Roasted red sweet pepper strips**

1

Thaw fish, if frozen. Rinse fish; pat dry with paper towels. Brush fish with lime juice. Rub fish with red pepper and salt.

2

Lightly grease the unheated rack of a broiler pan. Place fish on rack. Broil 4 inches from heat for 8 to 12 minutes or just until fish flakes easily with a fork, carefully turning once halfway through broiling.

3

Meanwhile, in a small bowl combine mayonnaise dressing or salad dressing and honey mustard. Spread some of the mixture on cut sides of flatbread pieces. Place watercress or lettuce on bottom halves of flatbread pieces. Top with fish. Top fish with the remaining mayonnaise dressing mixture and sweet pepper strips. Add top halves of flatbread pieces.

Nutrition Facts per serving: 331 calories, 9 g total fat, 47 mg cholesterol, 522 mg sodium, 42 g carbohydrate, 21 g protein.

***Note:** If you like, substitute 4 kaiser rolls for the Italian flatbread.

POACHED ORANGE ROUGHY WITH LEMON SAUCE

The lemon-and-pepper-seasoned poaching liquid for the fish does double duty when it's transformed into a delicate chive sauce.

Start to Finish: 20 minutes **Makes:** 4 servings

- **1 pound fresh or frozen orange roughy or red snapper fillets, about 1/2 inch thick**
- **1 14-ounce can reduced-sodium chicken broth**
- **2 teaspoons finely shredded lemon peel**
- **1/8 teaspoon ground black pepper**
- **1 pound fresh asparagus spears, trimmed and cut in half**
- **1 medium yellow sweet pepper, cut into thin, bite-size strips**
- **4 teaspoons cornstarch**
- **2 tablespoons snipped fresh chives**
- **2 cups hot cooked couscous or rice**

1

Thaw fish, if frozen. Rinse fish; pat dry with paper towels. Cut fish into 4 serving-size pieces.

2

In a 10-inch skillet combine 1 cup of the broth, the lemon peel, and black pepper. Bring to boiling; reduce heat. Carefully add the fish and asparagus. Cover and cook over medium-low heat for 4 minutes. Add sweet pepper strips. Cover and cook about 2 minutes more or just until fish flakes easily with a fork. Using a slotted spatula, remove fish and vegetables from skillet, reserving liquid in skillet. Cover fish and vegetables to keep warm.

3

For sauce, in a bowl stir together the remaining broth and the cornstarch. Stir into liquid in skillet. Cook and stir until thickened and bubbly. Cook and stir for 2 minutes more. Stir in chives.

4

To serve, place fish and vegetables on couscous; top with sauce.

Nutrition Facts per serving: 249 calories, 2 g total fat, 60 mg cholesterol, 390 mg sodium, 29 g carbohydrate, 28 g protein.

CRISPY ORANGE ROUGHY WITH DILLED YOGURT SAUCE

Here's a dynamite health-conscious alternative to traditional fried fish.

Prep: 20 minutes **Bake:** 4 minutes **Makes:** 4 servings

- **1 pound fresh or frozen orange roughy or other fish fillets, 1/2 to 3/4 inch thick**
- **Nonstick cooking spray**
- **1/4 cup cornmeal**
- **1/2 teaspoon dried thyme, crushed**
- **1/4 teaspoon lemon-pepper seasoning**
- **1 egg white**
- **2 tablespoons water**
- **1/4 cup fine dry bread crumbs**
- **2 tablespoons toasted wheat germ**
- **1 tablespoon snipped fresh parsley**
- **1/2 teaspoon paprika**
- **1 8-ounce carton plain fat-free yogurt**
- **1/4 cup lemon fat-free yogurt**
- **1 teaspoon dried dill**
- **Few dashes bottled hot pepper sauce**
- **Lemon wedges (optional)**

1

Thaw fish, if frozen. Rinse fish; pat dry with paper towels. Cut fish into 4 serving-size pieces. Measure the thickness of fish. Coat a shallow baking pan with nonstick cooking spray; set aside.

2

In a shallow dish combine cornmeal, thyme, and lemon-pepper seasoning. In another shallow bowl beat egg white and the water until frothy. In a third shallow bowl combine bread crumbs, wheat germ, parsley, and paprika. Dip fish pieces into cornmeal mixture, shaking off any excess. Dip into egg white, then coat with bread crumb mixture.

3

Place fish pieces in prepared baking pan, tucking under any thin edges for an even thickness. Bake in a 450°F oven just until fish flakes easily with a fork (allow 4 to 6 minutes per 1/2-inch thickness of fish).

4

Meanwhile, for sauce, in a small bowl stir together plain yogurt, lemon yogurt, dill, and hot pepper sauce.

5

To serve, spoon sauce over fish. If desired, serve with lemon wedges.

Nutrition Facts per serving: 221 calories, 3 g total fat, 62 mg cholesterol, 271 mg sodium, 20 g carbohydrate, 29 g protein.

SWEET MUSTARD HALIBUT

Just three ingredients work fabulous flavor magic on these halibut steaks.

Start to Finish: 20 minutes **Makes:** 4 servings

1 to 1¼ pounds fresh or frozen halibut steaks, cut ¾ inch thick
½ cup chunky salsa
2 tablespoons honey
2 tablespoons Dijon-style mustard

1

Thaw fish, if frozen. Rinse fish; pat dry with paper towels. Measure the thickness of the fish. Arrange fish in a shallow 2-quart baking dish. Bake, uncovered, in a 450°F oven for 6 to 9 minutes or just until fish flakes easily with a fork. Drain liquid from fish.

2

Meanwhile, in a small bowl stir together the salsa and honey. Spread mustard over drained fish; spoon salsa mixture on top of mustard. Bake for 2 to 3 minutes more or until mustard and salsa mixture are hot.

Nutrition Facts per serving: 176 calories, 4 g total fat, 36 mg cholesterol, 362 mg sodium, 11 g carbohydrate, 24 g protein.

COD WITH LEMON CREAM SAUCE

Low in both calories and fat, fish makes the ideal centerpiece for a healthful menu. Round out the meal with the spinach fettuccine, crusty bread, and low-fat or fat-free ice cream for dessert.

Start to Finish: 20 minutes **Makes:** 4 servings

- **1 pound fresh or frozen cod or other fish fillets, 1/2 to 3/4 inch thick**
- **1 1/2 cups water**
- **1 tablespoon lemon juice**
- **1/2 cup finely chopped carrot**
- **1/2 cup finely chopped onion**
- **1/2 cup fat-free milk**
- **1 teaspoon cornstarch**
- **1/2 teaspoon instant chicken bouillon granules**
- **1 teaspoon snipped fresh dill or 1/4 teaspoon dried dill**
- **Hot cooked spinach fettuccine or medium noodles (optional)**

1

Thaw fish, if frozen. Rinse fish; pat dry with paper towels. Tuck under any thin edges of fish for an even thickness.

2

In a 12-inch skillet combine the water and lemon juice. Bring to boiling. Add fish. Cover and simmer for 4 to 8 minutes or just until fish flakes easily with a fork. Remove fish from skillet; cover to keep warm.

3

Meanwhile, in a small covered saucepan cook carrot and onion in a small amount of boiling water about 3 minutes or until crisp-tender. Drain well. In a small bowl combine milk, cornstarch, bouillon granules, and dill. Stir into vegetables in saucepan. Cook and stir until thickened and bubbly. Cook and stir for 2 minutes more.

4

To serve, if desired, arrange fish on top of hot cooked fettuccine. Spoon vegetable mixture over fish.

Nutrition Facts per serving: 114 calories, 1 g total fat, 45 mg cholesterol, 199 mg sodium, 5 g carbohydrate, 20 g protein.

FISH FILLETS AND CAPONATA-STYLE VEGETABLES

Caponata is a Sicilian relish that can vary from area to area and cook to cook, but it usually starts with eggplant and onion.

Start to Finish: 25 minutes **Makes:** 4 servings

- **12 ounces fresh or frozen fish fillets (such as cod, haddock, or orange roughy)**
- **Nonstick cooking spray**
- **1/2 of a small eggplant, peeled and chopped (about 1 1/2 cups)**
- **1/2 cup chopped red or green sweet pepper**
- **1/3 cup chopped onion**
- **1 clove garlic, minced**
- **1 small tomato, chopped**
- **1/4 cup water**
- **1/2 teaspoon dried oregano or basil, crushed**
- **2 tablespoons nonfat Italian salad dressing**
- **8 1/2-inch slices French bread, toasted**
- **Basil leaves (optional)**

1

Thaw fish, if frozen. Rinse fish; pat dry with paper towels. Cut into serving-size pieces. Coat a large nonstick skillet with nonstick cooking spray. Preheat over medium heat. Add eggplant, sweet pepper, onion, and garlic. Cook and stir for 4 minutes. Add tomato, the water, and oregano or basil. Cover and cook for 1 to 2 minutes more or until vegetables are tender. Remove from heat. Stir in 1 tablespoon of the salad dressing. Set aside.

2

Meanwhile, measure the thickness of fish. Coat the unheated rack of a broiler pan with nonstick cooking spray. Place fish on rack. Broil 4 inches from the heat just until fish flakes easily with a fork (allow 4 to 6 minutes per 1/2-inch thickness of fish).

3

To assemble, drizzle bread slices with remaining 1 tablespoon salad dressing. For each serving, place 1 fish fillet portion on top of 2 bread slices. Spoon some of the eggplant mixture over fish. If desired, garnish with basil leaves.

Nutrition Facts per serving: 230 calories, 2 g total fat, 36 mg cholesterol, 424 mg sodium, 32 g carbohydrate, 20 g protein.

OVEN-FRIED FISH

Turn this crispy fish into a sandwich by serving it in a kaiser roll with the tomato slices. If you like, add some fat-free mayonnaise dressing or salad dressing.

Prep: 15 minutes **Bake:** 4 minutes **Makes:** 4 servings

4 4-ounce fresh or frozen cod or other fish fillets
Nonstick cooking spray
3 tablespoons seasoned fine dry bread crumbs
3 tablespoons cornmeal
1/4 teaspoon lemon-pepper seasoning
1 tablespoon cooking oil
1 slightly beaten egg white
Tomato slices (optional)
Fresh parsley sprigs (optional)

1

Thaw fish, if frozen. Rinse fish; pat dry with paper towels. Measure thickness of fish. Coat a shallow baking pan with nonstick cooking spray. Set aside.

2

In a small bowl combine bread crumbs, cornmeal, and lemon-pepper seasoning. Add oil, tossing to combine. Brush 1 side of each fish fillet with the egg white, then dip in bread crumb mixture. Place fish fillets, crumb sides up, in prepared pan.

3

Bake, uncovered, in a 450°F oven just until fish flakes easily with a fork (allow 4 to 6 minutes per 1/2-inch thickness of fish). If desired, serve with tomato slices and garnish with parsley sprigs.

Nutrition Facts per serving: 161 calories, 5 g total fat, 43 mg cholesterol, 283 mg sodium, 9 g carbohydrate, 20 g protein.

SALMON WITH FRESH PINEAPPLE SALSA

Serve this tropical salmon with a tossed spinach salad dressed with light Italian salad dressing. *(Pictured on page 151.)*

Prep: 20 minutes **Grill:** 8 minutes **Makes:** 4 servings

- **1 1-pound fresh or frozen skinless salmon fillet, about 1 inch thick**
- **2 cups coarsely chopped fresh pineapple**
- **1/2 cup chopped red sweet pepper**
- **1/4 cup finely chopped red onion**
- **3 tablespoons lime juice**
- **1 small fresh jalapeño pepper,* seeded and finely chopped**
- **1 tablespoon snipped fresh cilantro or fresh chives**
- **1 tablespoon honey**
- **1/4 teaspoon ground cumin**
- **Fresh pineapple wedges (optional)**

1

Thaw fish, if frozen. Rinse fish; pat dry with paper towels. For salsa, in a medium bowl combine the chopped pineapple, sweet pepper, red onion, 2 tablespoons of the lime juice, the jalapeño pepper, cilantro or chives, and honey. Set aside. Brush both sides of fish with the remaining lime juice; sprinkle with cumin.

2

Well grease a wire grill basket. Place fish in grill basket, tucking under any thin edges for an even thickness. Place grill basket on the rack of an uncovered grill. Grill fish directly over medium coals for 8 to 12 minutes or just until fish flakes easily with a fork, carefully turning once halfway through grilling.

3

To serve, cut fish into 4 serving-size pieces. If desired, serve fish pieces on pineapple wedges. Spoon salsa over fish.

Nutrition Facts per serving: 170 calories, 4 g total fat, 20 mg cholesterol, 70 mg sodium, 17 g carbohydrate, 17 g protein.

***Note:** Because chile peppers, such as jalapeños, contain volatile oils that can burn your skin and eyes, avoid direct contact with them as much as possible. When working with chile peppers, wear plastic or rubber gloves. If your bare hands do touch the chile peppers, wash your hands and nails well with soap and water.

BROILED FISH STEAKS WITH TARRAGON CHEESE SAUCE

All it takes is yogurt, cheese, and tarragon for this simple but spectacular sauce. For extra punch, sprinkle on some cracked black pepper.

Start to Finish: 20 minutes **Makes:** 4 servings

- **1¼ pounds fresh or frozen salmon, swordfish, or tuna steaks, cut ¾ inch thick**
- **½ cup plain yogurt or light dairy sour cream**
- **½ cup shredded mozzarella or Monterey Jack cheese (2 ounces)**
- **2 teaspoons snipped fresh tarragon or ½ teaspoon dried tarragon, crushed**
- **Salt**
- **Ground black pepper**
- **Hot cooked bow ties or other pasta (optional)**
- **Fresh tarragon sprigs (optional)**
- **Red sweet pepper strips (optional)**

1

Thaw fish, if frozen. Rinse fish; pat dry with paper towels. If necessary, cut fish steaks into 4 equal portions.

2

In a bowl combine the yogurt or sour cream, cheese, and snipped or dried tarragon. Set aside.

3

Place fish on unheated rack of broiler pan. Sprinkle fish with salt and black pepper. Broil 4 inches from the heat for 6 to 9 minutes or just until fish flakes easily with a fork. Spoon yogurt mixture over fish steaks. Broil 30 to 60 seconds more or until heated through and cheese starts to melt.

4

To serve, if desired, arrange fish on hot cooked pasta and garnish with fresh tarragon sprigs and red pepper strips.

Nutrition Facts per serving: 188 calories, 8 g total fat, 36 mg cholesterol, 236 mg sodium, 3 g carbohydrate, 25 g protein.

PARMESAN BAKED FISH

Round out your menu by adding steamed broccoli and rice to this slimming, delicious salmon.

Prep: 15 minutes **Bake:** 12 minutes **Makes:** 4 servings

4 4-ounce fresh or frozen skinless salmon fillets or other firm fish fillets, 3/4 to 1 inch thick
Nonstick cooking spray
1/4 cup light mayonnaise dressing or salad dressing
2 tablespoons grated Parmesan cheese
1 tablespoon snipped fresh chives or sliced green onion
1 teaspoon white wine Worcestershire sauce
Fresh whole chives (optional)

1

Thaw fish, if frozen. Rinse fish; pat dry with paper towels. Coat a 2-quart square or rectangular baking dish with nonstick cooking spray. Set aside.

2

In a small bowl stir together mayonnaise dressing or salad dressing, Parmesan cheese, the snipped chives or sliced green onion, and the Worcestershire sauce. Spread mayonnaise mixture over fish fillets.

3

Bake, uncovered, in a 450°F oven just until fish flakes easily with a fork (allow 4 to 6 minutes per 1/2-inch thickness of fish). If desired, garnish with whole chives.

Nutrition Facts per serving: 169 calories, 10 g total fat, 23 mg cholesterol, 247 mg sodium, 1 g carbohydrate, 18 g protein.

DILLY SALMON FILLETS

This Scandinavian-influenced salmon boasts a dill and mustard mayonnaise topper.

Prep: 15 minutes **Marinate:** 10 minutes **Grill:** 11 minutes **Makes:** 4 servings

4 6-ounce fresh or frozen skinless salmon fillets, about 3/4 inch thick
3 tablespoons lemon juice
2 tablespoons snipped fresh dill
2 tablespoons mayonnaise or salad dressing
2 teaspoons Dijon-style mustard
Dash ground black pepper
Shredded cucumber (optional)

1

Thaw fish, if frozen. Rinse fish; pat dry with paper towels. Place fish in a shallow dish. In a small bowl combine the lemon juice and 1 tablespoon of the dill; pour over fish. Marinate in the refrigerator for 10 minutes. Meanwhile, in a small bowl stir together the remaining dill, the mayonnaise or salad dressing, mustard, and pepper; set aside.

2

Lightly grease the grill rack of a covered grill. In the grill arrange medium-hot coals around a drip pan. Test for medium heat above pan. Place fish on the greased grill rack over the drip pan. Cover and grill for 5 minutes. Turn fish; spread with the mayonnaise mixture. Cover and grill for 6 to 9 minutes more or until fish flakes easily with a fork.

3

To serve, if desired, arrange fish on shredded cucumber.

Nutrition Facts per serving: 211 calories, 11 g total fat, 35 mg cholesterol, 204 mg sodium, 1 g carbohydrate, 25 g protein.

ASIAN GLAZED SALMON FILLETS

Grilling with indirect heat in a covered grill helps keep the sweet-sour glaze from burning.

Prep: 10 minutes **Grill:** 14 minutes **Makes:** 2 servings

2 5-ounce fresh or frozen skinless, boneless salmon fillets, about 1 inch thick
2 tablespoons bottled sweet-and-sour sauce
1 teaspoon hot Chinese mustard
1 teaspoon finely grated fresh ginger
Hot cooked soba noodles (buckwheat noodles) (optional)
Slivered pea pods, steamed (optional)
Pink or black peppercorns, cracked (optional)

1

Thaw fish, if frozen. Rinse fish; pat dry with paper towels. For glaze, in a small bowl combine sweet-and-sour sauce, mustard, and ginger; mix well. Brush fish with glaze. Discard any remaining glaze.

2

In a grill with a cover arrange medium-hot coals around a drip pan. Test for medium heat above the pan. Place fish, skinned sides down, on a grill rack over pan. Cover and grill for 14 to 18 minutes or just until fish flakes easily with a fork.

3

To serve, if desired, toss together soba noodles and pea pods. Arrange fish on noodle mixture. If desired, sprinkle with cracked peppercorns.

Nutrition Facts per serving: 155 calories, 5 g total fat, 25 mg cholesterol, 169 mg sodium, 6 g carbohydrate, 20 g protein.

SAUTÉED SHRIMP WITH PEPPERS

For a change of pace, serve this fruity shrimp over fragrant, nutty basmati or jasmine rice. You'll find them in the rice section of larger supermarkets or in food specialty stores.

Start to Finish: 25 minutes **Makes:** 2 servings

- **8 ounces fresh or frozen shrimp in shells**
- **Nonstick cooking spray**
- **2 small red and/or green sweet peppers, cut into thin, bite-size strips**
- **1/4 cup sliced green onions**
- **1 clove garlic, minced**
- **1/2 of an 8-ounce can (1/2 cup) sliced water chestnuts, drained**
- **2 tablespoons apricot preserves**
- **1 tablespoon light or regular soy sauce**
- **Several dashes bottled hot pepper sauce**
- **1 cup hot cooked rice or orzo (rosamarina)**
- **1 teaspoon sesame seeds, toasted**

1

Thaw shrimp, if frozen. Peel and devein shrimp. Rinse shrimp; pat dry with paper towels. Coat an unheated medium skillet with nonstick cooking spray. Heat skillet over medium heat. Cook sweet peppers, green onions, and garlic in hot skillet for 3 to 4 minutes or until tender.

2

Add shrimp and water chestnuts. Cook and stir for 3 to 4 minutes or until shrimp turn opaque. Remove from heat. Stir in apricot preserves, soy sauce, and hot pepper sauce.

3

To serve, spoon shrimp mixture over hot cooked rice or orzo. Sprinkle with sesame seeds.

Nutrition Facts per serving: 220 calories, 2 g total fat, 131 mg cholesterol, 436 mg sodium, 34 g carbohydrate, 17 g protein.

SHRIMP-ARTICHOKE FRITTATA

A frittata is terrific anytime—for breakfast or brunch, as a light lunch, or for a speedy supper.

Start to Finish: 30 minutes **Makes:** 4 to 6 servings

- **4 ounces fresh or frozen shrimp in shells**
- **1/2 of a 9-ounce package frozen artichoke hearts**
- **2 cups refrigerated or frozen egg product, thawed**
- **1/4 cup fat-free milk**
- **1/4 cup thinly sliced green onions**
- **1/8 teaspoon garlic powder**
- **1/8 teaspoon ground black pepper**
- **Nonstick cooking spray**
- **3 tablespoons finely shredded Parmesan cheese**
- **Cherry tomatoes, quartered (optional)**
- **Fresh parsley sprigs (optional)**

1

Thaw shrimp, if frozen. Peel and devein shrimp. Rinse shrimp; pat dry with paper towels. Halve shrimp lengthwise; set aside. Meanwhile, cook artichoke hearts according to package directions; drain. Cut artichoke hearts into quarters; set aside.

2

In a bowl combine egg product, milk, green onions, garlic powder, and pepper; set aside.

3

Lightly coat an unheated large nonstick skillet with nonstick cooking spray. Heat skillet. Cook shrimp in hot skillet for 1 to 3 minutes or until shrimp turn opaque.

4

Pour egg mixture into skillet; do not stir. Place skillet over medium-low heat. As the egg mixture sets, run a spatula around the edge of the skillet, lifting egg mixture so uncooked portion flows underneath. Continue cooking and lifting edge until mixture is almost set but still glossy and moist.

5

Remove skillet from heat; sprinkle artichoke pieces evenly over the top. Sprinkle with Parmesan cheese. Cover and let stand for 3 to 4 minutes or until top is set.

6

To serve, loosen edge of frittata. Transfer to a serving plate; cut into wedges. If desired, garnish with cherry tomatoes and parsley.

Nutrition Facts per serving: 126 calories, 3 g total fat, 37 mg cholesterol, 343 mg sodium, 6 g carbohydrate, 19 g protein.

PASTA WITH SPICY SHRIMP SAUCE

Basil, dried tomatoes, garlic, and crushed red pepper make this easy sauce bold and flavorful.

Start to Finish: 30 minutes **Makes:** 8 servings

- 1½ pounds fresh or frozen peeled and deveined shrimp (with tails intact, if desired)
- 2 tablespoons olive oil or cooking oil
- 2 cups sliced fresh mushrooms
- 2 small onions, cut into thin wedges
- 3 cloves garlic, minced
- 2 10-ounce cans chopped tomatoes and green chile peppers
- ½ cup snipped oil-packed dried tomatoes, drained
- ⅓ cup snipped fresh basil
- 1 bay leaf
- ¼ teaspoon crushed red pepper
- 1 pound dried fettuccine or linguine
- Fresh basil sprigs (optional)
- Olives (optional)

1

Thaw shrimp, if frozen. Rinse shrimp; pat dry with paper towels. Halve large shrimp lengthwise.

2

In a large skillet heat oil. Cook mushrooms, onions, and garlic in hot oil for 4 to 5 minutes or until mushrooms are tender, stirring occasionally. Stir in undrained tomatoes with green chile peppers, dried tomatoes, snipped basil, bay leaf, and red pepper. Bring to boiling; reduce heat. Simmer, uncovered, for 5 to 15 minutes or until sauce thickens slightly.

3

Meanwhile, cook pasta according to package directions. Stir shrimp into tomato mixture. Return to boiling; reduce heat. Cover and simmer for 2 or 3 minutes or until shrimp turn opaque. Discard bay leaf.

4

To serve, drain pasta. Spoon sauce over pasta. If desired, garnish with basil sprigs and olives.

Nutrition Facts per serving: 358 calories, 6 g total fat, 131 mg cholesterol, 455 mg sodium, 52 g carbohydrate, 23 g protein.

DILLED SHRIMP WITH RICE

Stop by the supermarket and pick up some cooked, peeled shrimp and you can have this elegant entrée ready in next to no time.

Start to Finish: 25 minutes **Makes:** 4 servings

- **12 ounces fresh or frozen peeled, cooked shrimp with tails**
- **1½ cups shredded carrots**
- **⅔ cup thinly sliced leeks**
- **1 cup fresh pea pods, halved crosswise**
- **1 tablespoon margarine or butter**
- **1 teaspoon instant chicken bouillon granules**
- **¼ cup hot water**
- **2 cups hot cooked rice**
- **1 teaspoon finely shredded lemon peel**
- **1 tablespoon snipped fresh dill or ½ teaspoon dried dill**

1

Thaw shrimp, if frozen. In a large skillet cook and stir carrots, leeks, and pea pods in hot margarine or butter for 2 to 3 minutes or until vegetables are crisp-tender.

2

In a small bowl dissolve bouillon granules in the water. Stir shrimp, rice, lemon peel, and dissolved granules into skillet. Cook about 5 minutes or until heated through, stirring occasionally. Stir in dill.

3

To serve, divide rice mixture among 4 bowls.

Nutrition Facts per serving: 268 calories, 4 g total fat, 166 mg cholesterol, 478 mg sodium, 35 g carbohydrate, 22 g protein.

JALAPEÑO SHRIMP AND PASTA

If you like to add fire to lots of different foods, keep some sliced jalapeños on hand in your freezer. You don't need to thaw them before chopping or using in cooked dishes.

Start to Finish: 25 minutes **Makes:** 4 servings

- **12 ounces fresh or frozen shrimp in shells**
- **8 ounces dried penne (mostaccioli), rigatoni, or cavatelli**
- **1 medium onion, chopped**
- **1 small fresh jalapeño pepper,* seeded and finely chopped**
- **2 cloves garlic, minced**
- **1/4 teaspoon ground cumin**
- **1/4 teaspoon ground black pepper**
- **1/8 teaspoon salt**
- **1 tablespoon margarine or butter**
- **2 medium tomatoes, chopped**
- **1 4-ounce can diced green chile peppers, drained**
- **Fresh whole chile peppers (optional)**

1

Thaw shrimp, if frozen. Peel and devein shrimp. Rinse shrimp; pat dry with paper towels. Halve any large shrimp.

2

Cook pasta according to package directions. Drain pasta. Return to pan. Cover; keep warm. Meanwhile, in a 10-inch skillet cook and stir shrimp, onion, chopped jalapeño pepper, garlic, cumin, black pepper, and salt in hot margarine or butter for 1 to 3 minutes or until shrimp turn opaque. Gently stir in tomato and diced green chile peppers. Heat through.

3

To serve, top hot cooked pasta with shrimp mixture. If desired, garnish with whole chile peppers.

Nutrition Facts per serving: 345 calories, 5 g total fat, 131 mg cholesterol, 338 mg sodium, 51 g carbohydrate, 23 g protein.

***Note:** Because chile peppers, such as jalapeños, contain volatile oils that can burn your skin and eyes, avoid direct contact with them as much as possible. When working with chile peppers, wear plastic gloves. If your bare hands do touch the chile peppers, wash your hands well with soap and water.

PEPPY ASPARAGUS-SHRIMP TOSS

If you want to cook your own shrimp, start with 12 ounces of shrimp in the shell to get the 8 ounces cooked shrimp.

Start to Finish: 20 minutes **Makes:** 4 servings

- **8 ounces fresh or frozen peeled, cooked shrimp with tails**
- **8 ounces fresh asparagus, trimmed and cut into $1^1/_2$-inch pieces**
- **3 cups cooked brown rice, chilled**
- **3 tablespoons chopped oil-packed dried tomatoes, drained**
- **2 tablespoons sweet-hot mustard**
- **$^1/_4$ cup sliced almonds, toasted**
- **Coarsely ground black pepper (optional)**

1

Thaw shrimp, if frozen. In a covered saucepan cook asparagus in a small amount of boiling water for 3 to 6 minutes or until crisp-tender; drain. Rinse under cold water; drain again.

2

In a large bowl toss together asparagus, rice, shrimp, and tomatoes. Add mustard; toss lightly to coat.

3

To serve, divide mixture among 4 dinner plates. Sprinkle each serving with some of the almonds. If desired, sprinkle with pepper.

Nutrition Facts per serving: 306 calories, 7 g total fat, 111 mg cholesterol, 205 mg sodium, 42 g carbohydrate, 20 g protein.

PAN-SEARED SCALLOPS

Sea scallops are the largest variety of scallop. They are most plentiful from mid to late fall into spring. When you purchase them, choose firm, sweet-smelling ones.

Start to Finish: 20 minutes **Makes:** 4 servings

- **1 pound fresh or frozen sea scallops**
- **2 tablespoons all-purpose flour**
- **1 to 2 teaspoons blackened steak seasoning or Cajun seasoning**
- **1 tablespoon cooking oil**
- **1 10-ounce package prewashed fresh spinach**
- **1 tablespoon water**
- **2 tablespoons balsamic vinegar**
- **1/4 cup cooked bacon pieces**

1

Thaw scallops, if frozen. Rinse scallops; pat dry with paper towels. In a plastic bag combine flour and seasoning. Add scallops; toss to coat. In a large skillet heat oil. Cook scallops in hot oil over medium heat about 6 minutes or until browned and opaque, turning to brown evenly. Remove scallops.

2

Add spinach to skillet; sprinkle with the water. Cover and cook over medium-high heat about 2 minutes or just until spinach is wilted. Add vinegar; toss to coat evenly. Return scallops to skillet; heat through. Sprinkle with bacon.

Nutrition Facts per serving: 158 calories, 6 g total fat, 37 mg cholesterol, 323 mg sodium, 9 g carbohydrate, 18 g protein.

SUNSHINE SALAD

Golden summer fruits add "sunshine" to this shrimp and scallop medley.

Start to Finish: 20 Minutes **Makes:** 6 servings

- **1 recipe Ginger-Cream Dressing**
- **1 pound sea scallops, cooked and chilled***
- **8 ounces peeled, cooked shrimp with tails, chilled****
- **8 cups torn mixed salad greens**
- **1 large peach or nectarine or 2 apricots, pitted and sliced**
- **1 large mango or small papaya, peeled, pitted, and sliced**
- **2 tablespoons cashew halves or sliced almonds, toasted (optional)**

1

Prepare Ginger-Cream Dressing. In a large bowl toss scallops; shrimp; salad greens; peach, nectarine, or apricots; and mango or papaya with dressing until coated.

2

To serve, if desired, garnish with cashews or almonds.

Ginger-Cream Dressing: Stir together 1/2 cup fat-free dairy sour cream, 2 tablespoons finely chopped crystallized ginger, 1 tablespoon sherry vinegar, 1/2 teaspoon finely shredded orange peel, and dash ground red pepper. Stir in orange juice (about 2 tablespoons) as needed for desired consistency. Season to taste with salt. Makes about 2/3 cup.

Nutrition Facts per serving: 197 calories, 5 g total fat, 79 mg cholesterol, 459 mg sodium, 20 g carbohydrate, 20 g protein.

***Note:** To cook the scallops, cook them in 4 cups boiling, salted water for 2 to 3 minutes or until scallops turn opaque, stirring occasionally. Rinse under cold running water. Drain and chill in the refrigerator.

****Note:** You can purchase peeled, cooked shrimp at most seafood counters. However, if you prefer to cook your own, start with 12 ounces shrimp in the shell. Peel and devein shrimp. Cook shrimp in 4 cups boiling, salted water for 1 to 3 minutes or until shrimp turn opaque, stirring occasionally. Rinse under cold running water. Drain and chill in the refrigerator.

CURRIED CRAB SALAD

A light curry dressing makes this fruit and crab combo sure to please.

Start to Finish: 20 minutes **Makes:** 3 servings

- **6 ounces cooked crabmeat, cut into bite-size pieces, or one 6-ounce package frozen crabmeat**
- **2 cups cut-up fresh fruit (such as pineapple, cantaloupe, honeydew melon, strawberries, and/or whole raspberries)**
- **3/4 cup sliced celery**
- **1/4 cup light mayonnaise dressing or salad dressing**
- **1/4 cup plain low-fat yogurt**
- **2 tablespoons fat-free milk**
- **1/2 teaspoon curry powder**
- **4 cups torn mixed salad greens**

1

Thaw crabmeat, if frozen. In a large bowl combine crabmeat, fresh fruit, and celery; set aside.

2

For dressing, in a small bowl stir together mayonnaise dressing or salad dressing, yogurt, milk, and curry powder.

3

To serve, toss crab mixture with salad greens. Divide mixture among 3 dinner plates. Drizzle with dressing.

Nutrition Facts per serving: 200 calories, 9 g total fat, 58 mg cholesterol, 361 mg sodium, 17 g carbohydrate, 14 g protein.

MEATLESS

Pasta, beans, eggs, and cheese take center stage in these healthful, yet full-flavored, family pleasers.

Pasta with Ricotta and Vegetables
(see recipe, page 206)

PENNE WITH FENNEL

The mellow licorice flavor of the fennel adds an intriguing dimension to this pasta and bean dish.

Start to Finish: 30 minutes **Makes:** 4 servings

- **6 ounces dried penne (mostaccioli)**
- **2 medium fennel bulbs**
- **1 tablespoon olive oil or cooking oil**
- **1 tablespoon margarine or butter**
- **3 cloves garlic, minced**
- **1/4 teaspoon crushed red pepper**
- **1 cup red and/or green sweet pepper cut into thin, bite-size strips**
- **1 15-ounce can Great Northern beans, rinsed and drained**
- **1/4 teaspoon dried thyme, crushed**
- **Ground black pepper**
- **1/4 cup shaved or shredded Parmesan cheese**

1

Cook penne according to package directions. Drain penne. Return to pan. Cover; keep warm.

2

Cut off and discard upper stalks from fennel bulbs. If desired, reserve some of the feathery leaves for garnish. Cut fennel bulbs lengthwise into quarters. Remove and discard core. Cut fennel into thin strips.

3

In a large skillet heat oil and margarine or butter. Cook garlic in skillet over medium-high heat for

30 seconds. Add fennel and crushed red pepper; cook and stir for 5 minutes more. Add sweet pepper strips; cook for 3 minutes more. Add beans and thyme; cook about 2 minutes or until heated through.

4

To serve, add fennel mixture to hot cooked pasta; toss gently. Season to taste with black pepper. Serve with Parmesan cheese. If desired, garnish with reserved fennel leaves.

Nutrition Facts per serving: 349 calories, 9 g total fat, 5 mg cholesterol, 309 mg sodium, 53 g carbohydrate, 15 g protein.

SOUTHWESTERN BLACK BEAN CAKES WITH GUACAMOLE

Sizzling right from the grill, these Tex-Mex vegetarian burgers are delicious simply topped with guacamole and tomato or tucked into a kaiser roll or hamburger bun.

Prep: 20 minutes **Grill:** 8 minutes **Makes:** 4 servings

- **1/2 of a medium avocado, seeded and peeled**
- **1 tablespoon lime juice**
- **Salt**
- **Ground black pepper**
- **2 slices whole wheat bread, torn**
- **3 tablespoons fresh cilantro leaves**
- **2 cloves garlic**
- **1 15-ounce can black beans, rinsed and drained**
- **1 canned chipotle pepper in adobo sauce**
- **1 to 2 teaspoons adobo sauce**
- **1 teaspoon ground cumin**
- **1 egg**
- **1 small plum tomato, chopped**

1

For guacamole, in a small bowl mash avocado. Stir in lime juice; season to taste with salt and black pepper. Cover surface with plastic wrap and refrigerate until ready to serve.

2

Place torn bread in a food processor bowl or blender container. Cover and process or blend until bread resembles coarse crumbs. Transfer bread crumbs to a large bowl; set aside.

3

Place cilantro and garlic in the food processor bowl or blender container. Cover and process or blend until finely chopped. Add the beans, chipotle pepper, adobo sauce, and cumin. Cover and process or blend using on/off pulses until beans are coarsely chopped and mixture begins to pull away from side of bowl or container. Add bean mixture to bread crumbs. Add egg; mix well. Shape into four 1/2-inch patties.

4

Lightly grease the rack of an uncovered grill. Place patties on rack. Grill directly over medium coals for 8 to 10 minutes or until patties are heated through, turning once halfway through grilling.

5

To serve, top the patties with guacamole and tomato.

Nutrition Facts per serving: 178 calories, 7 g total fat, 53 mg cholesterol, 487 mg sodium, 25 g carbohydrate, 11 g protein.

PASTA WITH RICOTTA AND VEGETABLES

A bevy of vegetables makes this hearty pasta a real feast for the eyes and the palate. *(Pictured on page 201.)*

Start to Finish: 25 minutes **Makes:** 4 servings

- **8 ounces dried penne (mostaccioli) or cut ziti**
- **2 1/2 cups fresh broccoli florets**
- **1 1/2 cups fresh asparagus or green beans cut into 1-inch pieces**
- **2 large red and/or yellow tomatoes**
- **1 cup light ricotta cheese**
- **1/4 cup shredded fresh basil**
- **4 teaspoons snipped fresh thyme**
- **4 teaspoons balsamic vinegar**
- **1 tablespoon olive oil**
- **1 clove garlic, minced**
- **1/2 teaspoon salt**
- **1/2 teaspoon ground black pepper**
- **2 tablespoons grated Parmesan or Romano cheese**
- **Fresh thyme sprigs (optional)**
- **Shaved Parmesan or Romano cheese (optional)**

1

Cook pasta according to package directions, adding broccoli and asparagus or green beans for the last 3 minutes of cooking.

2

Meanwhile, place a fine strainer over a large bowl. Cut tomatoes in half; squeeze seeds and juice into strainer. With the back of a spoon, press seeds against strainer to extract juice; discard seeds. Coarsely chop tomatoes.

3

Add ricotta cheese, basil, snipped thyme, vinegar, oil, garlic, salt, and pepper to tomato juice; mix well. Stir in tomatoes.

4

To serve, drain pasta and vegetables; add to ricotta cheese mixture in bowl and toss well. Divide mixture among 4 bowls. Sprinkle with grated Parmesan or Romano cheese. If desired, garnish with thyme sprigs and shaved Parmesan or Romano cheese.

Nutrition Facts per serving: 368 calories, 8 g total fat, 12 mg cholesterol, 393 mg sodium, 57 g carbohydrate, 19 g protein.

THE CASUAL OMELET

A chive-seasoned omelet wrapped around a spinach and red pepper filling makes a satisfying entrée for brunch or an informal supper.

Start to Finish: 20 minutes **Makes:** 2 servings

1 recipe Red Pepper Relish
1 cup refrigerated or frozen egg product, thawed, or 4 eggs
1 tablespoon snipped fresh chives, flat-leaf parsley, or chervil
Dash salt
Dash ground red pepper
Nonstick cooking spray
1/4 cup shredded reduced-fat sharp cheddar cheese (1 ounce)
1 cup firmly packed torn fresh spinach
Lemon wedges (optional)

1

Prepare Red Pepper Relish. In a large bowl use a rotary beater or wire whisk to beat together the egg product or eggs; chives, parsley, or chervil; salt; and ground red pepper until frothy.

2

Coat an unheated 8-inch nonstick skillet with flared sides or a crepe pan with nonstick cooking spray. Preheat skillet over medium heat. Pour egg mixture into prepared skillet; cook over medium heat. As mixture begins to set, run a spatula around edge of skillet, lifting mixture so uncooked portion flows underneath.

3

When eggs are set but still glossy and moist, sprinkle with cheese. Top with three-fourths of the spinach and 2 tablespoons of the Red Pepper Relish. Fold one side of omelet partially over filling. Top with the remaining spinach and 1 tablespoon of the relish. (Reserve the remaining relish for another use.)

4

To serve, divide omelet in half and, if desired, serve with lemon wedges.

Red Pepper Relish: In a small bowl combine 1/3 cup chopped red sweet pepper, 1 tablespoon finely chopped onion, 1 1/2 teaspoons cider vinegar, and 1/8 teaspoon ground black pepper. Cover and store in the refrigerator for up to 3 days. Makes about 1/2 cup.

Nutrition Facts per serving: 121 calories, 3 g total fat, 10 mg cholesterol, 380 mg sodium, 7 g carbohydrate, 16 g protein.

WHOLE WHEAT LINGUINE WITH SPRING VEGETABLES

Seven different vegetables and spunky jalapeño pepper make this innovative pasta first-rate.

Start to Finish: 30 minutes **Makes:** 4 servings

- 6 ounces dried whole wheat linguine
- 2 teaspoons olive oil
- 2 large shallots, thinly sliced
- 1 teaspoon minced garlic
- 1 fresh jalapeño pepper,* seeded and finely chopped
- 3/4 cup thinly sliced celery
- 3/4 cup thinly sliced carrot
- 1 cup small broccoli florets
- 8 ounces fresh asparagus, trimmed and cut into 1-inch pieces
- 1 small zucchini, halved and thinly sliced
- 2 cups sliced fresh shiitake or button mushrooms
- 4 ounces fresh pea pods, trimmed and halved diagonally
- 3/4 cup vegetable broth or chicken broth
- 1/2 teaspoon salt
- 1/4 teaspoon ground black pepper
- 2 tablespoons snipped fresh chives
- Whole fresh chives (optional)

1

Cook linguine according to package directions. Drain linguine. Return to pan. Cover; keep warm. Meanwhile, in a large skillet heat oil over high heat. Cook shallots, garlic, and jalapeño pepper in hot oil about 1 minute or until shallots are soft.

2

Add the celery and carrot; cook and stir for 1 minute. Stir in the broccoli, asparagus, zucchini, mushrooms, pea pods, and broth. Cover and cook for 3 minutes.

3

Add the hot linguine, salt, and black pepper to the skillet; toss gently to combine with vegetables.

4

To serve, transfer the mixture to a serving bowl and sprinkle with snipped chives. If desired, garnish with whole chives.

Nutrition Facts per serving: 271 calories, 4 g total fat, 0 mg cholesterol, 475 mg sodium, 53 g carbohydrate, 12 g protein.

***Note:** Because chile peppers, such as jalapeños, contain volatile oils that can burn your skin and eyes, avoid direct contact with them as much as possible. When working with chile peppers, wear plastic or rubber gloves. If your bare hands do touch the chile peppers, wash your hands and nails well with soap and water.

TRATTORIA-STYLE SPINACH FETTUCCINE

This calorie- and fat-reduced fettuccine is so flavorful you'd expect to find it at a bistro.

Start to Finish: 20 minutes **Makes:** 4 servings

1 9-ounce package refrigerated spinach fettuccine
1 tablespoon olive oil
2 tablespoons chopped shallot or green onion
1 medium carrot, coarsely shredded (about 1/2 cup)
4 medium red and/or yellow tomatoes, coarsely chopped (about 1 1/4 pounds total)
1/4 cup oil-packed dried tomatoes, drained and snipped
1/2 cup crumbled garlic and herb or peppercorn feta cheese (2 ounces)

1

Using kitchen scissors, cut fettuccine strands in half crosswise. Cook the fettuccine according to package directions. Drain fettuccine. Return to pan. Cover; keep warm.

2

Meanwhile, in a large skillet heat oil. Cook shallot or green onion and carrots in hot oil over medium heat for 1 to 2 minutes or just until tender. Stir in chopped tomatoes and dried tomatoes; cook for 1 to 2 minutes or until heated through. Spoon tomato mixture over cooked fettuccine; toss gently.

3

To serve, divide fettuccine mixture among 4 bowls or 4 dinner plates. Sprinkle with cheese.

Nutrition Facts per serving: 311 calories, 11 g total fat, 72 mg cholesterol, 243 mg sodium, 44 g carbohydrate, 13 g protein.

TORTELLINI-VEGETABLE SALAD

Quick-to-fix refrigerated cheese tortellini tossed with greens, vegetables, and a homemade vinaigrette make for a captivating meatless meal that has only a smidge more than 300 calories a serving.

Start to Finish: 20 minutes **Makes:** 4 servings

- **1 9-ounce package refrigerated cheese tortellini**
- **6 cups torn mixed salad greens**
- **1½ cups sliced fresh mushrooms**
- **1 medium red sweet pepper, cut into thin, bite-size strips**
- **¼ cup snipped fresh basil**
- **¼ cup white wine vinegar or white vinegar**
- **2 tablespoons water**
- **2 tablespoons olive oil**
- **2 teaspoons sugar**
- **2 cloves garlic, minced**
- **¼ teaspoon ground black pepper**
- **½ cup fat-free toasted garlic-and-onion croutons**

1

In a large saucepan cook the tortellini according to package directions, except omit any oil or salt. Drain tortellini. Rinse with cold water; drain again.

2

In a large bowl combine tortellini, greens, mushrooms, sweet pepper, and basil.

3

For dressing, in a screw-top jar combine vinegar, the water, oil, sugar, garlic, and black pepper. Cover and shake well. Pour over tortellini mixture; toss to coat.

4

To serve, divide the tortellini mixture among 4 dinner plates. Top with the croutons.

Nutrition Facts per serving: 302 calories, 12 g total fat, 30 mg cholesterol, 288 mg sodium, 40 g carbohydrate, 12 g protein.

FONTINA AND MELON SALAD

For those torrid summer days when appetites lag, try this refreshing fruit salad.

Start to Finish: 25 minutes **Makes:** 4 servings

- **1½ cups dried large bow ties (farfalle) (about 6 ounces)**
- **2 cups cantaloupe and/or honeydew melon chunks**
- **1 cup cubed fontina or Swiss cheese (4 ounces)**
- **⅓ cup bottled fat-free poppy seed salad dressing**
- **1 to 2 tablespoons coarsely snipped fresh mint**
- **2 cups watercress, stems removed**
- **2 small cantaloupe or honeydew melons, halved and seeded (optional)**

1

Cook bow ties according to package directions. Drain bow ties. Rinse with cold water; drain again.

2

In a large bowl toss together bow ties, cantaloupe or honeydew melon chunks, and cheese. In a small bowl combine salad dressing and mint; pour over pasta mixture, tossing gently to coat. Serve immediately. (Or cover and chill in the refrigerator for up to 24 hours.)

3

To serve, stir watercress into pasta mixture. If desired, serve salad in melon shells.

Nutrition Facts per serving: 319 calories, 11 g total fat, 73 mg cholesterol, 309 mg sodium, 41 g carbohydrate, 14 g protein.

LENTIL AND VEGGIE TOSTADAS

Red lentils cook quickly, so you can enjoy these colorful tostadas almost anytime.

Start to Finish: 25 minutes **Makes:** 4 servings

- **1 3/4 cups water**
- **3/4 cup dry red lentils, rinsed and drained**
- **1/4 cup chopped onion**
- **1 to 2 tablespoons snipped fresh cilantro**
- **1/2 teaspoon salt**
- **1/2 teaspoon ground cumin**
- **1 clove garlic, minced**
- **4 tostada shells**
- **2 cups assorted chopped vegetables (such as broccoli, tomato, zucchini, and/or yellow summer squash)**
- **3/4 cup shredded Monterey Jack cheese (3 ounces)**

1

In a medium saucepan stir together the water, lentils, onion, cilantro, salt, cumin, and garlic. Bring to boiling; reduce heat. Cover and simmer for 12 to 15 minutes or until lentils are tender and most of the liquid is absorbed. Use a fork to mash the cooked lentils.

2

Spread lentil mixture on tostada shells; top with vegetables and cheese. Place on a large baking sheet. Broil 3 to 4 inches from the heat about 2 minutes or until cheese melts.

Nutrition Facts per serving: 288 calories, 11 g total fat, 20 mg cholesterol, 497 mg sodium, 34 g carbohydrate, 16 g protein.

FRUITED COTTAGE CHEESE SALAD

Tote this apple and dried fruit salad to work for lunch. Just be sure to keep it well chilled in a cooler.

Start to Finish: 15 minutes **Makes:** 1 serving

- **1/2 cup low-fat cottage cheese**
- **1 small apple, chopped**
- **2 tablespoons mixed dried fruit bits or raisins**
- **Dash ground cinnamon, ground nutmeg, or apple pie spice**
- **1 lettuce leaf**

1

In a small bowl stir together cottage cheese, apple, dried fruit bits or raisins, and cinnamon, nutmeg, or apple pie spice. Serve immediately. (Or cover and chill in the refrigerator for up to 24 hours.)

2

To serve, line a plate with lettuce leaf. Spoon cottage cheese mixture onto lettuce leaf.

Nutrition Facts per serving: 163 calories, 2 g total fat, 5 mg cholesterol, 380 mg sodium, 23 g carbohydrate, 15 g protein.

SIDE DISHES & DESSERTS

From stir-fried veggies to frosty sippers to fruit crisp, these snacks and sides are health-smart and fabulous.

Orange-Sauced Broccoli and Peppers
(see recipe, page 238)

CHOCOLATE-BANANA SHAKE

Kids love this shake—it makes a great after-school snack or before-bed treat.

Start to Finish: 10 minutes **Makes:** 6 servings

- **1½ cups vanilla fat-free yogurt**
- **1¾ cups fat-free milk**
- **1 small banana, cut into chunks**
- **½ of a 4-serving-size package fat-free instant chocolate pudding mix (about 5 tablespoons)**
- **6 fresh strawberries (optional)**
- **Grated chocolate (optional)**

1

In a blender container or food processor bowl combine the yogurt, milk, banana, and pudding mix. Cover and blend or process until smooth. If desired, garnish with strawberries and grated chocolate.

Nutrition Facts per serving: 115 calories, 0 g total fat, 2 mg cholesterol, 189 mg sodium, 24 g carbohydrate, 5 g protein.

PEACH SMOOTHIE

Need a way to convince your kids to drink their milk? Try this frosty, fruity sipper.

Start to Finish: 5 minutes **Makes:** 4 servings

- **2 fresh medium peeled peaches or unpeeled nectarines, quartered, or ½ of a 16-ounce package frozen unsweetened peach slices**
- **¾ cup fat-free milk**
- **¼ cup frozen orange-pineapple juice concentrate, thawed**
- **2 teaspoons sugar**
- **1 teaspoon vanilla**
- **1 cup ice cubes**

1

If desired, set aside 4 peach or nectarine slices for garnish. In a blender container combine the remaining peaches or nectarines, the milk, orange-pineapple juice concentrate, sugar, and vanilla. Cover and blend until smooth.

2

Gradually add ice cubes through hole in blender lid, blending until smooth after each addition. If desired, garnish with reserved peach or nectarine slices.

Nutrition Facts per serving: 70 calories, 0 g total fat, 1 mg cholesterol, 24 mg sodium, 15 g carbohydrate, 2 g protein.

STRAWBERRIES WITH LIME DIPPING SAUCE

Try this dipping sauce with some other popular fruits, such as apples, peaches, or pears.

Prep: 5 minutes **Makes:** 8 servings

- **1 8-ounce carton light or fat-free dairy sour cream**
- **2 tablespoons powdered sugar**
- **2 teaspoons finely shredded lime peel**
- **1 tablespoon lime juice**
- **3 cups small fresh strawberries (about 1 pint)**
- **Lime slices, halved (optional)**
- **Edible flowers (optional)**

1

For dipping sauce, in a small bowl stir together sour cream, powdered sugar, lime peel, and lime juice.

2

Wash strawberries but do not remove stems. Drain on several layers of paper towels. Serve berries with dipping sauce. If desired, garnish dip with lime slices and flowers.

Nutrition Facts per serving: 60 calories, 2 g total fat, 4 mg cholesterol, 33 mg sodium, 9 g carbohydrate, 2 g protein.

FRUITED SPINACH SALAD WITH CURRANT VINAIGRETTE

With only 46 calories and no fat per serving, this fruity spinach salad is a real nutrition bargain for the health conscious.

Start to Finish: 15 minutes **Makes:** 6 servings

- **1/4 cup currant jelly**
- **3 tablespoons red wine vinegar**
- **8 cups firmly packed fresh spinach leaves**
- **1 cup fresh strawberries, halved**
- **1 11-ounce can mandarin orange sections, drained**
- **4 green onions, sliced**

1

For vinaigrette, in a small saucepan combine currant jelly and vinegar. Cook and stir over medium-low heat just until jelly melts and mixture is smooth. Chill in the freezer for 10 minutes.

2

Meanwhile, in a large salad bowl combine spinach, strawberries, orange sections, and green onions. Drizzle vinaigrette over the spinach mixture; toss to coat.

Nutrition Facts per serving: 46 calories, 0 g total fat, 0 mg cholesterol, 72 mg sodium, 11 g carbohydrate, 2 g protein.

STIR-FRIED ASPARAGUS AND MUSHROOMS

Substitute dried dill or dried basil for the thyme whenever you like.

Start to Finish: 15 minutes **Makes:** 4 servings

- **1/3 cup water**
- **1 dried tomato (not oil packed), finely snipped**
- **1 teaspoon cornstarch**
- **1/2 teaspoon instant chicken bouillon granules**
- **1/4 teaspoon dried thyme, crushed**
- **Nonstick cooking spray**
- **1 pound fresh asparagus, trimmed and cut into 1-inch pieces (3 cups)**
- **1 1/2 cups sliced fresh mushrooms (4 ounces)**

1

In a small bowl stir together the water, tomato, cornstarch, bouillon granules, and thyme. Set aside.

2

Coat an unheated large skillet with nonstick cooking spray. Heat over medium heat. Stir-fry asparagus in the hot skillet for 4 minutes. Add the mushrooms; stir-fry for 1 1/2 minutes more.

3

Stir cornstarch mixture; add to vegetables in skillet. Cook and stir until thickened and bubbly. Cook and stir for 2 minutes more.

Nutrition Facts per serving: 36 calories, 1 g total fat, 0 mg cholesterol, 113 mg sodium, 6 g carbohydrate, 3 g protein.

CREAM-SAUCED PEAS AND ONIONS

Light cream cheese makes these peas rich, yet lower in fat than regular creamed peas.

Start to Finish: 10 minutes **Makes:** 5 servings

- **2 10-ounce packages frozen peas with pearl onions**
- **1/4 of an 8-ounce tub light cream cheese (about 1/4 cup)**
- **1 tablespoon fat-free milk**
- **1/8 teaspoon cracked black pepper**
- **1/8 teaspoon garlic powder**

1

Cook peas with pearl onions according to package directions. Drain well. Return peas and onions to the saucepan. Stir in the cream cheese, milk, pepper, and garlic powder. Cook and stir over medium heat until heated through.

Nutrition Facts per serving: 74 calories, 2 g total fat, 6 mg cholesterol, 105 mg sodium, 10 g carbohydrate, 4 g protein.

LEMON-TARRAGON VEGETABLES

Grilled or broiled pork, chicken, or fish is an ideal mealtime partner for these lemony herbed veggies.

Start to Finish: 25 minutes **Makes:** 4 servings

- **8 ounces large whole fresh mushrooms, halved or quartered**
- **2 small yellow summer squash or zucchini, halved lengthwise and cut into 1/2-inch slices**
- **1 medium onion, cut into wedges**
- **3/4 cup bias-sliced celery**
- **2 tablespoons chopped roasted red sweet pepper or pimiento**
- **1/2 teaspoon finely shredded lemon peel**
- **1 tablespoon lemon juice**
- **2 teaspoons snipped fresh tarragon or 1/4 teaspoon dried tarragon, crushed**

1

In a large covered saucepan cook mushrooms, squash, onion, and celery in a small amount of boiling water about 7 minutes or until vegetables are tender. Drain.

2

Return vegetables to saucepan. Stir in roasted red sweet pepper or pimiento, lemon peel, lemon juice, tarragon, and salt. Cook and stir about 1 minute more or until heated through.

Nutrition Facts per serving: 38 calories, 0 g total fat, 0 mg cholesterol, 91 mg sodium, 8 g carbohydrate, 2 g protein.

INDIAN-STYLE CAULIFLOWER

A nonstick skillet helps you keep cooking oil to a minimum when you stir-fry these spunky vegetables.

Start to Finish: 20 minutes **Makes:** 4 servings

- **1/2 teaspoon dry mustard**
- **1/4 teaspoon ground turmeric**
- **1/4 teaspoon ground cumin**
- **1/8 teaspoon ground coriander**
- **1/8 teaspoon ground red pepper**
- **1 tablespoon cooking oil**
- **4 cups cauliflower florets**
- **1 small red or green sweet pepper, cut into 1-inch pieces**
- **4 green onions, bias-sliced into 1-inch pieces**
- **1/4 cup chicken broth**

1

In a bowl combine the mustard, turmeric, cumin, coriander, and ground red pepper. Set aside.

2

Heat oil in a wok or large skillet over medium-high heat. (Add more oil if necessary during cooking.) Add cauliflower; stir-fry for 3 minutes. Add sweet pepper and green onions; stir-fry for 1 to 1 1/2 minutes. Reduce heat to medium. Add mustard mixture. Cook and stir for 30 seconds. Carefully stir in broth. Cook and stir about 1 minute more or until vegetables are heated through. Serve immediately.

Nutrition Facts per serving: 71 calories, 4 g total fat, 0 mg cholesterol, 58 mg sodium, 7 g carbohydrate, 3 g protein.

CARAMELIZED SWEET POTATOES

Low in fat but high in flavor, these brown sugar-glazed potatoes go with just about everything from pork chops to chicken to fish.

Start to Finish: 30 minutes **Makes:** 4 servings

- **2 large red or white onions, cut into 3/4-inch chunks**
- **4 teaspoons margarine or butter**
- **2 large sweet potatoes or yams, peeled and sliced 1/2 inch thick (about 1 pound)**
- **1/4 cup water**
- **2 tablespoons brown sugar**
- **3/4 teaspoon snipped fresh rosemary or 1/4 teaspoon dried rosemary, crushed**
- **Fresh rosemary sprigs (optional)**

1

In a large skillet cook onions in hot margarine or butter over medium-high heat for 3 to 4 minutes or until onions are nearly tender, stirring frequently. Stir in sweet potatoes or yams and the water. Cover and cook over medium heat for 10 to 12 minutes or until sweet potatoes are nearly tender, stirring occasionally.

2

Uncover skillet; add brown sugar and the snipped or dried rosemary. Cook, stirring gently, over medium-low heat for 4 to 5 minutes or until onions and sweet potatoes are glazed. If desired, garnish with fresh rosemary sprigs.

Nutrition Facts per serving: 173 calories, 4 g total fat, 0 mg cholesterol, 57 mg sodium, 33 g carbohydrate, 2 g protein.

ORANGE-SAUCED BROCCOLI AND PEPPERS

The combination of broccoli and sweet pepper makes an eye-catching serve-along for beef, pork, chicken, or fish. (Pictured on page 221.)

Start to Finish: 20 minutes **Makes:** 6 servings

- **3½ cups broccoli florets**
- **½ of a medium red sweet pepper, cut into thin, bite-size strips**
- **½ of a medium yellow sweet pepper, cut into thin, bite-size strips**
- **2 tablespoons finely chopped onion**
- **1 clove garlic, minced**
- **1 tablespoon margarine or butter**
- **1½ teaspoons cornstarch**
- **⅔ cup orange juice**
- **2 teaspoons Dijon-style mustard**

1

In a medium covered saucepan cook broccoli and sweet pepper in a small amount of boiling, lightly salted water about 8 minutes or until broccoli is crisp-tender; drain. Cover to keep warm.

2

Meanwhile, for sauce, in a small saucepan cook onion and garlic in hot margarine or butter over medium heat until onion is tender. Stir in cornstarch. Add orange juice and mustard. Cook and stir until mixture is thickened and bubbly. Cook and stir for 2 minutes more.

3

To serve, pour sauce over broccoli mixture. Toss gently to coat.

Nutrition Facts per serving: 58 calories, 2 g total fat, 0 mg cholesterol, 82 mg sodium, 8 g carbohydrate, 2 g protein.

SCONES WITH STRAWBERRY CREAM CHEESE

These golden wedges are best served warm, slathered with the berry-flavored spread.

Start to Finish: 30 minutes **Makes:** 10 scones

- **Nonstick cooking spray**
- **2 1/2 cups all-purpose flour**
- **1/4 cup sugar**
- **2 teaspoons baking powder**
- **1/8 teaspoon ground nutmeg**
- **2 tablespoons butter**
- **1/3 cup dried currants or raisins**
- **2/3 cup fat-free milk**
- **1 beaten egg**
- **1 egg white**
- **2 teaspoons fat-free milk**
- **1 recipe Strawberry Cream Cheese Spread**

1

Coat a baking sheet with nonstick cooking spray; set aside. In a medium bowl stir together flour, sugar, baking powder, and nutmeg. With a pastry blender, cut in butter until mixture resembles coarse crumbs. Stir in currants or raisins. Make a well in the center of the flour mixture. In a small bowl stir together the 2/3 cup milk, the egg, and egg white. Add milk mixture all at once to flour mixture. Using a fork, stir just until moistened.

2

Turn dough out onto a lightly floured surface. Quickly knead dough by folding and pressing gently for 10 to 12 strokes or until dough is smooth. Pat into a 9-inch circle; cut into 10 wedges. Transfer wedges to prepared baking sheet. Brush tops of scones with the 2 teaspoons milk.

3

Bake in a 450°F oven about 12 minutes or until light golden brown. Meanwhile, prepare Strawberry Cream Cheese Spread. Serve scones warm with spread.

Strawberry Cream Cheese Spread: In a blender container or food processor bowl combine 1/2 of an 8-ounce tub fat-free cream cheese and 3 tablespoons reduced-calorie strawberry preserves. Cover and blend or process until smooth. Makes 1/2 cup.

Nutrition Facts per scone: 195 calories, 3 g total fat, 24 mg cholesterol, 138 mg sodium, 34 g carbohydrate, 7 g protein.

BERRY-LEMON TRIFLE

Stop by the supermarket's bakery to pick up an angel food cake or bake one of your own.

Start to Finish: 15 minutes **Makes:** 4 servings

- **2 cups cubed angel food cake**
- **1 8-ounce carton lemon fat-free yogurt**
- **1/4 of an 8-ounce container frozen light whipped dessert topping, thawed**
- **1 cup mixed fresh berries (such as raspberries, blueberries, and sliced strawberries)**
- **Fresh mint sprigs (optional)**

1

Divide angel food cake cubes among 4 dessert dishes. In a small bowl combine the yogurt and whipped topping.

2

To serve, spoon the yogurt mixture on top of the cake cubes. Sprinkle with berries. If desired, garnish with mint sprigs.

Nutrition Facts per serving: 104 calories, 2 g total fat, 1 mg cholesterol, 152 mg sodium, 19 g carbohydrate, 3 g protein.

TIRAMISU

The original Italian classic dessert is known for being a real belt-buster. But this lighter version has the same great taste with only 155 calories and 5 grams of fat per wedge.

Prep: 25 minutes **Makes:** 16 servings

- **1 8-ounce package reduced-fat cream cheese (Neufchâtel), softened**
- **1/2 cup sifted powdered sugar**
- **3 tablespoons coffee liqueur**
- **1 8-ounce container light frozen whipped dessert topping, thawed**
- **1/4 cup fat-free dairy sour cream**
- **2 tablespoons coffee liqueur**
- **1 8- to 10-inch round angel food cake**
- **1/4 cup strong black coffee**
- **2 tablespoons coffee liqueur**
- **1 recipe Mocha Fudge Sauce (optional)**
- **Edible flowers (optional)**

1

For filling, in a large bowl combine the cream cheese, powdered sugar, and the 3 tablespoons liqueur. Beat with an electric mixer on medium speed until blended and smooth. Stir in 1/2 cup of the whipped dessert topping. Set aside.

2

For the frosting, in a medium bowl combine the remaining whipped dessert topping, the sour cream, and 2 tablespoons liqueur. Set aside.

3

Using a serrated knife, cut the angel food cake horizontally into 3 layers. Place 1 layer on a serving platter and the remaining 2 layers on large dinner plates. With a long-tined fork or a skewer, poke holes in the tops of all 3 layers.

4

In a small bowl combine the coffee and 2 tablespoons liqueur; drizzle over all layers. Spread the bottom layer with half of the filling. Add the middle layer and spread on the remaining filling. Add the top layer. Frost cake with the frosting. Serve immediately. (Or cover and chill in the refrigerator for up to 4 hours.)

5

To serve, if desired, prepare Mocha Fudge Sauce. Drizzle top and side of cake with sauce. Cut cake into wedges. If desired, garnish each serving with edible flowers.

Nutrition Facts per serving: 155 calories, 5 g total fat, 11 mg cholesterol, 203 mg sodium, 21 g carbohydrate, 3 g protein.

Mocha Fudge Sauce: In a small bowl dissolve 1 teaspoon instant coffee crystals in 1 teaspoon hot water; stir in 1/4 cup chocolate-flavored syrup.

CHOCOLATE RICOTTA-FILLED PEARS

Luscious ripe pears filled with a sweet chocolate-ricotta filling—now that's a little bit of heaven.

Start to Finish: 20 minutes **Makes:** 6 servings

- **1 cup ricotta cheese**
- **1/3 cup sifted powdered sugar**
- **1 tablespoon unsweetened cocoa powder**
- **1/4 teaspoon vanilla**
- **2 tablespoons miniature semisweet chocolate pieces**
- **1 teaspoon finely shredded orange peel**
- **3 large Bosc, Anjou, or Bartlett pears**
- **2 tablespoons orange juice**
- **2 tablespoons slivered or sliced almonds, toasted**
- **Fresh mint sprigs (optional)**
- **Orange peel curls (optional)**

1

In a medium bowl beat the ricotta cheese, powdered sugar, cocoa powder, and vanilla with an electric mixer on medium speed until combined. Stir in chocolate pieces and the shredded orange peel. Set aside.

2

Peel the pears; cut in half lengthwise and remove the cores. Remove a thin slice from the rounded side of each pear half so the halves will sit flat. Brush the pears all over with orange juice.

3

To serve, place the pear halves on 6 dessert plates. Spoon the ricotta mixture on top of the pears and sprinkle with almonds. If desired, garnish with mint sprigs and orange curls.

Nutrition Facts per serving: 166 calories, 6 g total fat, 13 mg cholesterol, 52 mg sodium, 24 g carbohydrate, 6 g protein.

GINGERED PEACH AND PEAR CRISP

You can keep the ingredients for this easy crisp on hand for a spur-of-the-moment dessert. Fresh ginger will last several months in your freezer.

Prep: 15 minutes **Bake:** 15 minutes **Makes:** 6 servings

1 16-ounce can peach slices (juice pack), drained
1 16-ounce can pear halves (juice pack), drained and cut up
1 teaspoon grated fresh ginger
½ cup finely crushed gingersnaps
½ cup quick-cooking rolled oats
2 tablespoons brown sugar

1

In an 8-inch quiche dish or 8×1½-inch round baking pan combine the peaches, pears, and fresh ginger.

2

In a small bowl stir together the gingersnaps, oats, and brown sugar. Sprinkle evenly over fruit. Bake in a 425°F oven for 15 to 20 minutes or until heated through.

Nutrition Facts per serving: 138 calories, 1 g total fat, 0 mg cholesterol, 48 mg sodium, 32 g carbohydrate, 2 g protein.

AUTUMN APPLE FRITTERS

No matter whether you enjoy them for dessert or as a snack, these crispy no-fuss fritters will hit the spot.

Start to Finish: 20 minutes **Makes:** 12 fritters

- **2 medium tart cooking apples (such as Jonathan or Granny Smith)**
- **2/3 cup all-purpose flour**
- **1 tablespoon powdered sugar**
- **1/2 teaspoon finely shredded lemon peel**
- **1/4 teaspoon baking powder**
- **1 egg**
- **1/2 cup milk**
- **1 teaspoon cooking oil**
- **Shortening or cooking oil for deep-fat frying**
- **Powdered sugar (optional)**

1

Core apples and cut each crosswise into 6 rings. In a medium bowl combine flour, the 1 tablespoon powdered sugar, the lemon peel, and baking powder.

2

In a bowl use a wire whisk to combine egg, milk, and the 1 teaspoon cooking oil. Add egg mixture all at once to flour mixture; beat until smooth.

3

Using a fork, dip apple rings into batter; drain off excess batter. Fry 2 to 3 rings at a time in deep hot fat (365°) about 2 minutes or until golden, turning once with a slotted spoon. Drain on paper towels. Repeat with remaining apple rings. If desired, sprinkle fritters with additional powdered sugar. Cool on wire racks.

Nutrition Facts per fritter: 91 calories, 6 g total fat, 19 mg cholesterol, 18 mg sodium, 9 g carbohydrate, 2 g protein.

INDEX

A-B

C-D

E-G

H-O

P-R

S-Z

Nutrition Facts:
How They're Calculated

The following criteria were used to calculate the nutrition facts given with each recipe in this book:

- Optional ingredients were omitted.
- When ingredient options are given (for example: ground beef or ground pork), the nutrition facts were calculated using the first option.
- Unless another type of milk is specifically listed, 2% reduced-fat milk was used in the calculations.
- If a range of servings is given, the nutrition facts were based on the lowest number of servings listed.

Emergency Substitutions

It you don't have:	Substitute:
Bacon, 1 slice, crisp-cooked, crumbled	1 tablespoon cooked bacon pieces
Baking powder, 1 teaspoon	½ teaspoon cream of tartar plus ¼ teaspoon baking soda
Balsamic vinegar, 1 tablespoon	1 tablespoon cider vinegar or red wine vinegar plus ½ teaspoon sugar
Bread crumbs, fine dry, ¼ cup	¾ cup soft bread crumbs, or ¼ cup cracker crumbs, or ¼ cup cornflake crumbs
Broth, beef or chicken, 1 cup	1 teaspoon or 1 cube instant beef or chicken bouillon plus 1 cup hot water
Butter, 1 cup	1 cup shortening plus ¼ teaspoon salt, if desired
Buttermilk, 1 cup	1 tablespoon lemon juice or vinegar plus enough milk to make 1 cup (let stand 5 minutes before using) or 1 cup plain yogurt
Chocolate, semisweet, 1 ounce	3 tablespoons semisweet chocolate pieces, or 1 ounce unsweetened chocolate plus 1 tablespoon granulated sugar, or 1 tablespoon unsweetened cocoa powder plus 2 teaspoons sugar and 2 teaspoons shortening
Chocolate, sweet baking, 4 ounces	¼ cup unsweetened cocoa powder plus ⅓ cup granulated sugar and 3 tablespoons shortening
Chocolate, unsweetened, 1 ounce	3 tablespoons unsweetened cocoa powder plus 1 tablespoon cooking oil or shortening, melted
Cornstarch, 1 tablespoon (for thickening)	2 tablespoons all-purpose flour
Corn syrup (light), 1 cup	1 cup granulated sugar plus ¼ cup water
Egg, 1 whole	2 egg whites, or 2 egg yolks, or ¼ cup refrigerated or frozen egg product, thawed
Flour, cake, 1 cup	1 cup minus 2 tablespoons all-purpose flour
Flour, self-rising, 1 cup	1 cup all-purpose flour plus 1 teaspoon baking powder, ½ teaspoon salt, and ¼ teaspoon baking soda
Garlic, 1 clove	½ teaspoon bottled minced garlic or ⅛ teaspoon garlic powder
Ginger, grated fresh, 1 teaspoon	¼ teaspoon ground ginger
Half-and-half or light cream, 1 cup	1 tablespoon melted butter or margarine plus enough whole milk to make 1 cup
Molasses, 1 cup	1 cup honey
Mustard, dry, 1 teaspoon	1 tablespoon prepared mustard (in cooked mixtures)
Mustard, prepared, 1 tablespoon	½ teaspoon dry mustard plus 2 teaspoons vinegar
Onion, chopped, ½ cup	2 tablespoons dried minced onion or ½ teaspoon onion powder
Sour cream, dairy, 1 cup	1 cup plain yogurt
Sugar, granulated, 1 cup	1 cup packed brown sugar or 2 cups sifted powdered sugar
Sugar, brown, 1 cup packed	1 cup granulated sugar plus 2 tablespoons molasses
Tomato juice, 1 cup	½ cup tomato sauce plus ½ cup water
Tomato sauce, 2 cups	¾ cup tomato paste plus 1 cup water
Vanilla bean, 1 whole	2 teaspoons vanilla extract
Wine, red, 1 cup	1 cup beef or chicken broth in savory recipes; cranberry juice in desserts
Wine, white, 1 cup	1 cup chicken broth in savory recipes; apple juice or white grape juice in desserts
Yeast, active dry, 1 package	about 2¼ teaspoons active dry yeast

Seasonings

Apple pie spice, 1 teaspoon	½ teaspoon ground cinnamon plus ¼ teaspoon ground nutmeg, ⅛ teaspoon ground allspice, and dash ground cloves or ginger
Cajun seasoning, 1 tablespoon	½ teaspoon white pepper, ½ teaspoon garlic powder, ½ teaspoon onion powder, ½ teaspoon ground red pepper, ½ teaspoon paprika, and ½ teaspoon ground black pepper
Herbs, snipped fresh, 1 tablespoon	½ to 1 teaspoon dried herb, crushed, or ½ teaspoon ground herb
Poultry seasoning, 1 teaspoon	¾ teaspoon dried sage, crushed, plus ¼ teaspoon dried thyme or marjoram, crushed
Pumpkin pie spice, 1 teaspoon	½ teaspoon ground cinnamon plus ¼ teaspoon ground ginger, ¼ teaspoon ground allspice, and ⅛ teaspoon ground nutmeg

Metric Information

The charts on this page provide a guide for converting measurements from the U.S. customary system, which is used throughout this book, to the metric system.

Product Differences

Most of the ingredients called for in the recipes in this book are available in most countries. However, some are known by different names. Here are some common American ingredients and their possible counterparts:

- Sugar (white) is granulated, fine granulated, or castor sugar.
- Powdered sugar is icing sugar.
- All-purpose flour is enriched, bleached or unbleached, white household flour. When self-rising flour is used in place of all-purpose flour in a recipe that calls for leavening, omit the leavening agent (baking soda or baking powder) and salt.
- Light-colored corn syrup is golden syrup.
- Cornstarch is cornflour.
- Baking soda is bicarbonate of soda.
- Vanilla or vanilla extract is vanilla essence.
- Green, red, or yellow sweet peppers are capsicums or bell peppers.
- Golden raisins are sultanas.

Volume and Weight

The United States traditionally uses cup measures for liquid and solid ingredients. The chart below shows the approximate imperial and metric equivalents. If you are accustomed to weighing solid ingredients, the following approximate equivalents will be helpful.

- 1 cup butter, castor sugar, or rice = 8 ounces = ½ pound = 250 grams
- 1 cup flour = 4 ounces = ¼ pound = 125 grams
- 1 cup icing sugar = 5 ounces = 150 grams

Canadian and U.S. volume for a cup measure is 8 fluid ounces (237 ml), but the standard metric equivalent is 250 ml.

1 British imperial cup is 10 fluid ounces.

In Australia, 1 tablespoon equals 20 ml, and there are 4 teaspoons in the Australian tablespoon.

Spoon measures are used for smaller amounts of ingredients. Although the size of the tablespoon varies slightly in different countries, for practical purposes and for recipes in this book, a straight substitution is all that's necessary. Measurements made using cups or spoons always should be level unless stated otherwise.

Common Weight Range Replacements

Imperial / U.S.	Metric
½ ounce	15 g
1 ounce	25 g or 30 g
4 ounces (¼ pound)	115 g or 125 g
8 ounces (½ pound)	225 g or 250 g
16 ounces (1 pound)	450 g or 500 g
1¼ pounds	625 g
1½ pounds	750 g
2 pounds or 2¼ pounds	1,000 g or 1 Kg

Oven Temperature Equivalents

Fahrenheit Setting	Celsius Setting*	Gas Setting
300°F	150°C	Gas Mark 2 (very low)
325°F	160°C	Gas Mark 3 (low)
350°F	180°C	Gas Mark 4 (moderate)
375°F	190°C	Gas Mark 5 (moderate)
400°F	200°C	Gas Mark 6 (hot)
425°F	220°C	Gas Mark 7 (hot)
450°F	230°C	Gas Mark 8 (very hot)
475°F	240°C	Gas Mark 9 (very hot)
500°F	260°C	Gas Mark 10 (extremely hot)
Broil	Broil	Grill

*Electric and gas ovens may be calibrated using celsius. However, for an electric oven, increase celsius setting 10 to 20 degrees when cooking above 160°C. For convection or forced air ovens (gas or electric), lower the temperature setting 25°F/10°C when cooking at all heat levels.

Baking Pan Sizes

Imperial / U.S.	Metric
9×1½-inch round cake pan	22- or 23×4-cm (1.5 L)
9×1½-inch pie plate	22- or 23×4-cm (1 L)
8×8×2-inch square cake pan	20×5-cm (2 L)
9×9×2-inch square cake pan	22- or 23×4.5-cm (2.5 L)
11×7×1½-inch baking pan	28×17×4-cm (2 L)
2-quart rectangular baking pan	30×19×4.5-cm (3 L)
13×9×2-inch baking pan	34×22×4.5-cm (3.5 L)
15×10×1-inch jelly roll pan	40×25×2-cm
9×5×3-inch loaf pan	23×13×8-cm (2 L)
2-quart casserole	2 L

U.S. / Standard Metric Equivalents

⅛ teaspoon = 0.5 ml

¼ teaspoon = 1 ml

½ teaspoon = 2 ml

1 teaspoon = 5 ml

1 tablespoon = 15 ml

2 tablespoons = 25 ml

¼ cup = 2 fluid ounces = 50 ml

⅓ cup = 3 fluid ounces = 75 ml

½ cup = 4 fluid ounces = 125 ml

⅔ cup = 5 fluid ounces = 150 ml

¾ cup = 6 fluid ounces = 175 ml

1 cup = 8 fluid ounces = 250 ml

2 cups = 1 pint = 500 ml

1 quart = 1 litre